Trade Governance of the Belt and Road Initiative

This book looks at the rationale behind the Belt and Road Initiative by China, and attempts to explain the motivation from economical and historical perspectives. The book also compares trade governance of China with those of the United Kingdom and United States, and analyzes the value construction and promotion process of Chinese trade governance.

Dawei Cheng is Professor at the Department of Economics at Renmin University of China, China.

Routledge Focus on Business and Management

The fields of business and management have grown exponentially as areas of research and education. This growth presents challenges for readers trying to keep up with the latest important insights. Routledge Focus on Business and Management presents small books on big topics and how they intersect with the world of business research.

Individually, each title in the series provides coverage of a key academic topic, whilst collectively, the series forms a comprehensive collection across the business disciplines.

Stories for Management Success
The Power of Talk in Organizations
David Collins

How to Resolve Conflict in Organizations
The Power of People Models and Procedure
Annamaria Garden

Branding and Positioning in Base of Pyramid Markets in Africa
Innovative Approaches
Charles Blankson, Stanley Coffie and Joseph Darmoe

Persuasion
The Hidden Forces that Influence Negotiations
Jasper Kim

Trade Governance of the Belt and Road Initiative
Economic Logic, Value Choices, and Institutional Arrangement
Dawei Cheng

For more information about this series, please visit: www.routledge.com/
Routledge-Focus-on-Business-and-Management/book-series/FBM

Trade Governance of the Belt and Road Initiative

Economic Logic, Value Choices, and Institutional Arrangement

Dawei Cheng

LONDON AND NEW YORK

First published 2018
byRoutledge
2 Park Square, Milton Park, Abingdon, Oxon OX14 4RN

and by Routledge
605 Third Avenue, New York, NY 10017

First issued in paperback 2020

Routledge is an imprint of the Taylor & Francis Group, an informa business

British Library Cataloguing-in-Publication Data
A catalogue record for this book is available from the British Library

Library of Congress Cataloging-in-Publication Data
A catalog record for this book has been requested

ISBN 13: 978-0-367-50433-5 (pbk)
ISBN 13: 978-1-138-57266-9 (hbk)

Typeset in Times New Roman
by Apex CoVantage, LLC

Contents

Illustrations

Figures

Tables

1 Trade governance of the Belt and Road Initiative

Economic logic, value choices, and institutional arrangement

Introduction

Regression of globalization and the global governance crisis

Globalization greatly promotes the rapid flow of resources on a global scale, as well as the development of international trade and international investments. However, it has also exacerbated numerous global problems. The call for global governance by the international community strengthens every day, and coordination and cooperation are crucial in resolving these problems.

Western scholars believe that economic globalization originated in the United Kingdom, stating that, essentially, the British capitalist model of production is a globalized method and economic globalization and the capitalist model of production are synchronous. Between the end of the 19th century and beginning of the 20th century, global governance emerged amidst the development of globalization, the most prominent phenomenon being the rise of international organizations such as the League of Nations. After World War II, globalization entered a new phase of development with the rise of key international organizations such as the United Nations (UN) and World Trade Organization (WTO). During this period, governance became a key agenda in the international community. However, when researching the Belt and Road Initiative (B&R), and particularly when attempting to apply the concepts of the B&R in the world of 2,000 years ago, it becomes apparent that the history of globalization extends beyond that of capitalist globalization. China began trading with its neighboring countries as early as the Han dynasty and developed a crude governance model to manage trade relations. Therefore, the history of globalization should be traced back 2,000 years to identify globalization in the agriculture-pasturing period and uncover ancient global governance systems.

After two millennia of globalization, severe setbacks have recently occurred, fueled by the United Kingdom European Membership (or "Brexit") referendum in 2016 and the inauguration of the Trump administration in the United States in 2017. The first document concerning trade issued by the Trump administration in 2017 publically held the WTO in contempt, thereby driving global trade governance into its most severe state of crisis to date. Therefore, understanding how to view anti-globalization campaigns and save global trade governance is imperative. In a time of reverse globalization, superior global governance is needed.

Research content

Global governance is currently in a state of rapid transformation. Amidst the restructuring of American policies, the international community increasingly expects China to become the new mainstay of globalization. Specific targets are examined when analyzing global trade governance to highlight governance problems in global trade systems (e.g., value, regulation, and enforcement). In this book, we examine China's B&R to elucidate the characteristics of Chinese trade governance theories.

Academic research has initiated a discussion regarding China's involvement in global trade governance since its proposal of the B&R. Making special contributions toward global trade governance could be beneficial to China if it can epitomize the B&R experience. This book concentrates on four aspects of the B&R, detailed as follows:

1   Historical premise of the B&R: This book analyzes the historical evolution of globalization, causes of current reverse globalization phenomena, and characteristics of various globalization periods. Finally, China's B&R missions in relation to global trade governance are deduced.
2   Economic logic of the B&R: By promoting policy coordination, facility connectivity, unimpeded trade, financial integration, and people-to-people bonds as the five major B&R cooperation areas, the B&R connects China with other countries along the Belt and Road. The B&R enables these countries to participate in the international division of labor, create more cooperation opportunities in the region, and explore new development patterns, the logic behind which is to cultivate the value chain and expand the area of traditional trade to intra-industry trade and intra-product trade, thereby achieving the goal of "unimpeded trade."
3   The values and goals of B&R as a part of the global trade governance: The Belt and Road Initiative is put forward in the background of reverse globalization, with the historical mission to sustain the global balance

and integrate the countries that used to be marginalized in the process of globalization into the new globalization system. The new globalization system is supposed to promote the common development among countries and therefore it will also be the economic target of China's trade governance. B&R puts forward the concepts of "community of shared destiny" and "win–win," which mark the formation of China's values on global governance.

4   Implementation of the B&R: Rather than constituting a new form of trade negotiation, the B&R is a policy advocating economic cooperation and an innovation of policy advocacy methods in global governance. China provides innovative methods to advance the B&R by aligning the development strategies of all countries along the Belt and Road in an open manner. China can implement the multilateralization aspect of the B&R and gain international legal status for the B&R through multilateral diplomatic activities.

Research significance

Examining the trade governance of China's B&R has positive theoretical and practical implications.

Regarding the practical implications, China's position on global governance has sequentially evolved from one of conservatism and opposition to one of acceptance and active inquisition. After assuming office, President Xi Jinping emphasized the value of global governance research. Since the proposal and implementation of the B&R, China has introduced a number of new terms associated with global governance, such as "connectivity" and "three communities of common destiny." Collectively, these terms form China's unique ideology on global governance. This book analyzes B&R governance practices in China and examines China's involvement in global trade governance not only to enhance understanding of China but also to consolidate the governance experiences of other countries to improve China's governance capability.

Regarding the theoretical implications, China advocates a world of *mei-meiyu gong*, where people of different ethnical backgrounds should appreciate not only their own culture but also those of other ethnicities – an ideology that stems from China's ancient philosophies and wisdom. By contrast, the Trump administration proposed the "America First" foreign policy as a solution to the stagnation of globalization. This contrast raises two questions: (1) What is the theoretical logic behind these two governance ideologies? (2) Which of China's efforts to promote global trade governance reform through the B&R or the "America First" foreign policy proposed by the Trump administration is more effective? China launched the B&R as a promotional initiative to be fulfilled through bilateral or regional integration. This initiative generates several key questions, specifically: (1) What are the differences between B&R negotiations and those of the Regional Comprehensive Economic Partnership (RCEP) and Trans-Pacific Partnership (TPP) previously advocated by the United States? (2) What are the challenges of global trade governance? (3) How does B&R governance overcome the challenges of global trade governance? All of these governance issues will be discussed in the book.

Methodological innovation

This book adopts several research methods, the first of which is **historical research**. The author combed through the trade governance ideologies of ancient China and those adopted during the American and British hegemonic eras to describe changes in the global trade system. Limited resources hindered forming comprehensive observations based on all relevant historical data. Nonetheless, examining changes in globalization and problems of global governance from a historical perspective can facilitate the making of future predictions.

During the composition of this book, I made a unique observation. The historical research method considers problems as a whole rather than addressing them individually. Once an overall evaluation of all observed problems has been obtained, the relations between individual elements can be identified. So the historical research method considers the holistic course of development between specific events rather than considering individual points in time. This observation leads to the second research method adopted.

The second method adopted in this book is **holistic analysis**. This book analyzes global systems as a whole to provide readers with a holistic view of global trade governance. Therefore, "observing the world from a world perspective" is one of the analysis methods adopted. Once this sentiment has been achieved, we can fully understand the intricacies of Hegel's philosophy. The concept of "totalitarianism" (or "holism" or "entirety") is a fundamental concept in Hegel's philosophy. Hegel strongly advocated this concept, explaining that unsystematic philosophizing lacks scientific credibility. Unsystematic philosophies are typical expressions of subjective views with coincidental content. Only content that serves as a segment of an overall ideology can be accurately validated. The entirety of the global trade system is expressed as its existence as a system, or as a set of values, rules, processes, and mechanisms of global trade. As parts of a whole, these values, processes, and rules have unique characteristics. However, in the process of system development, the content maintains coherence with the system, composing the content and characteristics of the system during the period in question. In other words, all principles are included in and among themselves, serving as elements that contribute to global trade as a whole.

Hegel's philosophy concerns the transformation of partial or individual elements into a whole. Entities exist as special provisions or elements, and each entity is a whole in itself. Countries such as the United Kingdom, United States, and China have formulated unique theories of trade governance based on their own cultures and systemic characteristics. Therefore, these countries are independent entities. Entities become a whole when the entities and whole share common content, which is intrinsic proof of the existence of the whole. The global trade system can exist because it shares common content and logical requirements with its constituent parts (e.g., countries). We believe that this commonality is the basis for the creation of systems and derives the core concept of win–win cooperation.

This book explores the global trade system as a whole and in relation to its parts by analyzing the system while considering that each country therein is an independent sovereign entity. In addition, this book considers harmony and differences between individual parts while analyzing global systems as wholes. Analyzing global systems from the perspective of holism is the novelty of this book. The research methods adopted herein diverge from mainstream methods adopted by Western scholars that focus on entities.

The third method adopted in this book is **process theory**. Many studies on the philosophies of "process" have been published. The theory of "thesis, antithesis, and synthesis" developed by Hegel classifies all processes into three stages, specifically (1) similarity that exists in the origin or beginning of development, or thesis; (2) the emergence of opposition, or antithesis; and (3) the merging of thesis and antithesis, or synthesis. During the composition of this book, Donald Trump was inaugurated as president of the United States, serving as an illustration of how the rise of reverse globalization initiated the "antithesis" stage of globalization. When we examined globalization, we did not completely deny globalization or free trade but rather explored why "antitheses" occurred throughout history. Our solution to "antithesis" is "synthesis," indicating that the historical mission of the B&R was to assist globalization in entering the "synthesis" stage to restore global equilibrium.

In reality, processes are an element of time. Incorporating time into the holistic analysis of trade governance is similar to mapping two-dimensional coordinates in a three-dimensional space, which would substantially alter the layout of the coordinates. When observations are focused on individual entities, each entity sees only itself, and this can lead to policies such as "America First" being proposed. By contrast, when we consider the whole, we see other entities and perceive their relationships with us. When we consider others, we are better able to realize the concept of "win–win." When we look to the future, we realize the underlying wisdom and value of willingness. While analyzing the "win–win" concept of the B&R's introduction in China, we supplemented the concept of willingness, which means willing to pay first and gain in the future.

From the perspectives of entirety and time, we validated that events and systems are opposing and symbiotic wholes and the interrelationships between all entities in a system are continuously changing. Global systems are not clearly defined or mutually exclusive; they are wholes undergoing continuous change. The relationships that constitute a whole repeatedly interact and change during development. The evolution from relational associations to codependent ones is the primary goal of the global community. This book analyzes global trade governance from a global perspective. Resolving conflicts of interest between countries is an urgent concern of global trade governance.

The fourth method adopted in this book is **interdisciplinary research**. The content of this book encompasses the fields of economics, international politics (diplomacy), law, and philosophy. Global governance theory is an interdisciplinary theory; therefore, we adopted an interdisciplinary approach to analyzing global governance.

2 Globalization

The precondition of global trade governance

Logical relations between globalization and global governance

In his book *The World Is Flat*, Thomas L. Friedman classifies globalization into three time phases, described as follows. Globalization 1.0 began with Columbus discovering the New World in 1492 and ended before the British industrial revolution in the 1800s. Globalization 2.0 began with the industrial revolution and ended in the year 2000. Globalization 3.0 began in the year 2000. Friedman states that the three phases involved different driving forces and dominant factors. Specifically, in Globalization 1.0, the primary driving forces and dominant factors were "a country's strength" and "imperialism." In Globalization 2.0, the driving force was multinational corporations. In Globalization 3.0, the driving force is information technology. Friedman's timeline of globalization is extremely helpful in that it characterizes the relationship between the development of productivity and globalization and clearly highlights the promotional effects of the industrial revolution on globalization. Moreover, Friedman's classification identifies the protagonists of globalization in different periods. In Globalization 1.0, the dominant country was the United Kingdom, which promoted globalization through imperial expansion and the spread of capitalism. In Globalization 2.0, the dominant country was the United States, which promoted globalization through the global allocation of resources by American companies after the second industrial revolution. Friedman believes that information technology will shape global production and outsourcing will become more prevalent, thereby integrating more countries into the global production system and forming what he calls a "flat earth." However, although Friedman proposes a robust history of globalization, he fails to predict the occurrence of reverse globalization.

American economist Richard Baldwin is an influential scholar in the fields of globalization and global trade governance. Baldwin categorized post–industrial revolution globalization into two major stages and subsequently developed numerous substages based on regulations and statuses of global trade policies. Baldwin maintained that before the industrial revolution, production and consumption were largely region specific, and thus international trade and trade rules were of little consequence. The industrial revolution lifted the regional constraints on production and consumption for the first time; Baldwin termed this phenomenon "the great unbundling" and asserted that it greatly enhanced the importance of international trade. Thus far, the "unbundling" process has gone through three stages. The first stage was the great separation of production and consumption, which began with the British industrial revolution and ended with the advent of World War II. In this stage, transportation reform greatly reduced the transportation costs of trains and automobiles, engendering the first "great unbundling" of production and consumption and the rapid development of international trade. However, global trade was largely unregulated during this period and lacked a set of universal regulations. The second stage began at the end of World War II and ended in the early 21st century. In this stage, the "unbundling" of regional production and consumption continued to intensify and trade achieved rapid expansion, leading to an unprecedented international business revolution. The regulation of international trade occurred concurrently with this revolution and trade was placed under the governance of multilateral trade systems such as the General Agreement on Tariffs and Trade (GATT) and later the World Trade Organization (WTO). The third stage began at the beginning of the 21st century and is referred to as the "new unbundling" stage. The primary characteristics of this stage are the rapid development of intra-product trade and global value chain division and increased intra-region and intra-industry chain associations between companies. This new stage of globalization yields new challenges, particularly that of the "governance gap" in the global economy. Baldwin asserted that the multilateral trade system established by the WTO to address old goods and service–based trade issues was inadequate for coping with the new stage. In reality, global economic governance is currently experiencing a dangerous governance gap.

The study of globalization development is the study of productivity, encompassing technological reform, flow of capital, and production paradigms. The study of trade governance is the study of production relationships, encompassing relationships between entities in global systems, institutional arrangements, and the evolution of regulations. Changes in global governance stem from the development of globalization.

As mentioned, Western scholars believe that economic globalization originated in the United Kingdom, stating that essentially, the British capitalist model of production is a globalized method and economic globalization and the capitalist model of production are synchronous. This concept raises the question of whether globalization existed prior to capitalist globalization.

The ancient Silk Road: globalization during the agriculture-pasturing period

The Silk Road refers to the ancient trade route between China and the Mediterranean. The route promoted initial trade and exchanges of religion between Africa, Europe, Asia, and China, thereby promoting globalization during the agriculture-pasturing period. The Silk Road was a multinational trade route that enabled people of isolated tribes and settlements to primarily trade local goods transported by camels and mules in an unproductive yet self-sufficient economy based on agriculture and animal husbandry.

The Silk Road in the Han dynasty

During the Western Han dynasty between 138 and 119 BC, Envoy Zhang Qian led two expeditions west. Starting from Chang'an (known today as Xi'an), Zhang established trade with numerous Central Asian countries such as Afghanistan, Iran, Iraq, and Syria before eventually reaching Rome, thereby creating a 6,440-kilometer land trade route. At that time, the world was controlled by four major empires, namely the Han, Roman, Parthian, and Kushan Empires. These empires coexisted while occupying different regions and maintaining distinct cultures. The Silk Road connected the four empires for the first time, thereby constituting the first occurrence of globalization in human history.

The Kushan Empire comprised the area from present-day Tajikistan to the Caspian Sea, Afghanistan, and the Indus Valley, thereby controlling most of Central Asia. The Kushans were primarily agricultural people who farmed wheat, grapes, and grains. In regions unsuitable for farming, people largely reared cows, sheep, goats, horses, and camels. The Kushans were well known for their horses by the Han. The Kushan Empire had an active trade system, where trade between agricultural and nomadic regions was extremely active; crops, fruit, handicrafts, and weapons from agricultural regions were traded to nomadic regions for furs, cattle, textiles, meat, and dairy products. The Silk Road intersected the Kushan Empire, enabling Kushan merchants to serve as middlemen. Kushan merchants traveled north to Southern Asia, east to the central plains, and west to the Roman Empire, transporting spices and luxury goods from the Silk Road to India and Rome and bringing Roman weapons back east. China received grapes, pomegranates, and walnuts from Central Asia.

Agriculture was a principal component of the Roman economy. The main products were wheat, olives, and grapes, with olives and grapes being the most prominent crops in the Mediterranean region. Rome primarily produced pottery and Spain had a well-developed mining industry. Regarding textiles, Padova's woolen fabric, Spain's woolen cloaks, and Gaul's hooded coats were extremely popular. Spain also produced fish sauce that was used as seasoning for cooking.

The Parthian Empire was an Iranian Empire in West Asia that practiced slavery. During its most prosperous period, the Parthian Empire spanned north to the Euphrates in Southeast Anatolia and east to the Amu Darya. Parthia was essential for the expansion of the Silk Road and the empire benefited from transit trade. To maintain mutual interests, Parthia and China maintained a positive relationship; for example, ancient Chinese texts describe how the Parthian Empire once dispatched a troupe to China to perform acrobatics and magic for the Han people.

The Silk Road spanned four empires and constituted the first international trade system between China, Central Asia, the Middle East, and Europe. In an era of feudalism and slavery, the Silk Road was established and maintained by the determination of several countries and their rulers, as well as merchants, laborers, and monks. Therefore, the Silk Road exhibited a two-tier trade system consisting of intergovernmental trade and the more widespread activity of civilian trade.

On his first expedition, Zhang Qian passed through regions referred to in Chinese chronicles as Dawan (now the Fergana Basin, Uzbekistan), Kangju (now Syr Darya, northeast Kazakhstan and parts of Uzbekistan), Dayuezhi (now parts of the Amu Darya, Turkmenistan, and northern Afghanistan), and Daxia (now Afghanistan), all of which were borders to ancient western civilizations. The Egyptian, Mesopotamian, Indian, Persian, Greek, and northern grassland civilizations had previously converged, integrated, collided, and developed in these regions. The arrival of Zhang connected eastern and western civilizations, which subsequently converged. Today, we can see, regarding religion, Islam of the Parthian Empire, Christianity of the Roman Empire, Buddhism of the Kushan Empire, and Confucianism of the Chinese Empire were cultivated and developed on the Silk Road. This was the first time in history that the world's major civilizations collided.

In summary, the Silk Road interconnected several civilizations, all of which valued learning, production, labor, and the acquisition of knowledge and wealth, and these values facilitated the longevity of the Silk Road. During the Han and Tang dynasties, the empires involved on the Silk Road were open and enterprising empires. The Romans, Persians, Arabs, Han Chinese, and Han-Tang Chinese were all proud and confident people, and this mentality compelled these empires to value and support trade on the Silk Road.

In addition, foreign products and cultures were accepted by these empires and their rulers. More crucially, the Silk Road facilitated the establishment of diplomatic channels from China to Central and Western Asia, Europe, and Africa. The Silk Road enabled China to expand its influence internationally for the first time.

The Maritime Silk Road

Trade was established on land and at sea during the Han dynasty. The Maritime Silk Road extended across the Indian Ocean to the Bay of Bengal.

Up until the mid-Tang dynasty, China's efforts and resources had been centered on economic development in the north. However, after the An Lushan Rebellion, the Tang Empire began to shift its focus toward Jianghuai in the south, paying particular attention to maritime trade in Guangzhou. These efforts gave rise to the China Road, where China established trade with Southeast Asian countries in the South China Sea. Therefore, the Maritime Silk Road was in use for over two millennia, originating during the Western Han dynasty, prospering during the Tang, Song, and Yuan dynasties, and eventually declining after the imposition of the *Haijin* (sea ban on private foreign trade) during the Ming dynasty.

Government support for the Silk Road

China introduced a number of policies to facilitate the development and continuity of the Silk Road during the Han dynasty, such as intermarriage and the development of management systems. China respected the sovereignty of all countries involved on the Silk Road, accepting the various political management systems, militaries, and ranking systems of other countries so long as they gained the acknowledgment of the imperial Chinese court in the form of offerings. To form and maintain relationships with prominent and influential countries, the Han government adopted the *heqin* (marriage alliance) policy, which saw imperial princesses betrothed to princes of neighboring countries to establish alliances. Regarding routine management, the Han dynasty relied on the western regions to maintain unity and attract and help smaller countries in handling local affairs. A support system was created by establishing stations along the Silk Road that provided accommodation and transport to ensure fluid trade. To ensure the supply of water along the Silk Road, the Han government centered efforts on maintaining the sustainability of the water networks in the Qilian Mountains while appropriately developing and applying water resources. The water conservancy construction of Hexi began during the Han period.

Tributary trade and the tributary system

Tributary trade was a traditional form of trade on the Silk Road. During the Tang dynasty, tributary trade was the primary trade model of the Tang government and the northern and western minorities of Central Asia; over a course of 154 years (618–772), the northern and western minorities of Central Asia paid tribute to the Tang dynasty 134 times. Tributary trade eventually evolved into a more systematic governance arrangement known as the ancient Chinese tributary system. This system was centered on China and encompassed numerous neighboring countries and minority regimes. With trade as the catalyst, a series of formal and informal external systems and regulations were formed. Tributary trade was a key trade model that differed from previous trade models on the Silk Road in the following manners. First, tributary trade was a model adopted by governments of various countries to fulfill their trade responsibilities. Second, tributary trade involved only China's neighboring countries, which were only a small number of the countries involved on the Silk Road; if the Silk Road exhibited globalization characteristics, the tributary system exhibited only localization characteristics. Third, the Silk Road was sufficiently robust to enable more than only tributary trade, also accommodating civilian merchant trade, which promoted the exchange of products between empires and between China and its neighboring countries to a greater extent than did tributary trade. Fourth, tributary trade promoted diplomacy. Tributary trade was deemed the global governance model of ancient China and reflected the diplomatic philosophy and institutional arrangement of the ancient Chinese government.

Fundamentally, analyzing China's model of tributary trade involves examining its trade governance. The tributary trade system was an ideal system characterized by Confucian beliefs. Confucianism advocates that people should strive to maintain benevolence, there by promoting global benevolence and attracting people to China. The tributary system implies that the governance of ancient China was based on "courtesy" rather than "force." This system was conceived under a natural, agriculture-based economy. Tributary trade was a behavioral model based on China's Confucian culture to maintain foreign relations. It was an ethical model that deemed military involvement unconventional, instead emphasizing the ethical establishment of harmony and order. Therefore, tributary trade can also be considered ethical idealism. In this manner, tributary trade set the governance ideologies of ancient China apart from those of other civilizations.

Civilian trade on the Silk Road

Rather than being based on the "pure business activity" principle of market economics, the Silk Road was a by-product of China's efforts to establish political ties through governance, the military, and economic policies. Nonetheless, an abundance of civilian trade occurred on the Silk Road.

Civilian trade on the Silk Road was primarily conducted by civilian merchants. Influential merchants formed caravans for long-distance trading. Generally, caravans comprised people of multiple ethnicities and the composition of the participants was extremely complex. Most caravans had hybrid organizational structures of two or more ethnicities. In addition to farmers, highly mobile nomads constituted large proportions of the Central Asian, Western Asian, and Roman populations in caravans. Ethnic groups maintained exchange relationships with one another, thereby contributing to the complexity of caravan compositions. Caravans operating on the Silk Road were required to travel across many regions with different rulers. Having local people in a caravan who were familiar with local customs and local natural environments was essential for ensuring safe passage. In summary, hybrid organizational structures were a key feature of civilian , caravans.

Monks who preached their religion were common companions of international traders on the Silk Road. These two types of travelers were reliant on and benefited from each other while traveling on the treacherous and dangerous road; traders provided resources for monks and received mental support in return. Although their objectives were different, monks and traders maintained a relationship based on mutual benefits. This partnership was extremely beneficial for the spread of religion.

Many markets on the Silk Road were "exchange" or "trading" markets. Competent traders from numerous ethnic groups established trading posts along the road that were vital to merchants as locations not only for business but also for the recuperation of their caravans.

Revelations of the Silk Road

The Silk Road reflected interconnection between ancient civilizations and the joint promotion of regional development. First and foremost, the Silk Road promoted market connectivity, connecting independent markets through trade. In addition, the Silk Road promoted migration, investment, and cultural exchange through trade. Native products were the primary items of trade on the Silk Road. Therefore, trade was based around the natural resources of different countries. During the Han dynasty, new tools and methods for developing products were gradually introduced to lagging regions along the Silk Road. Foreign crops were introduced and grown in substantial quantities, production tools were imitated and applied, and medical practices introduced from foreign regions were applied to treat people and animals, thereby indirectly enhancing the life expectancy and production enthusiasm of impoverished people and fueling the economic development of neighboring countries. The all-around economic advancement of the Han Empire became a positive example for many nomadic nations, objectively promoting economic development in neighboring countries.

Second, the Silk Road not only strengthened production and cultural exchanges among numerous countries en route but also generated a spillover effect for the first globalized system. Western countries anticipated acquiring knowledge and experience for advancement from the Han Empire. This situation marked the dispersion and infiltration of the "spillover effect." After the launch of the Silk Road, the road gradually gained recognition in western countries, which increasingly sought to learn the etiquette of the Han dynasty.

Third, the Silk Road enabled the coexistence of military and economic diplomacy. "Peaceful" diplomacy was valued on the Silk Road, and this created the opportunity for economic diplomacy to become prevalent. The objective of Zhang Qian's expedition to the west was to defeat the Huns through close combat and distant diplomacy. This became a classic military diplomacy tactic. However, economic diplomacy gradually became the mainstream method employed by countries along the Silk Road; for example, the Han dynasty adopted the *heqin* policy to reinforce its borders and promote agricultural – pastoral reciprocity through orderly immigration. Therefore, we speculate that the rise of the Silk Road was the first occurrence of globalization in human history, occurring in the agricultural-pastoral era. With the rise of the United Kingdom, the world entered an era of imperial colonialism and capitalist globalization on a larger scale. During this new era of blood and war, China's tributary system gradually shifted toward recession.

Globalization in the Anglo-American era

Globalization and the British Empire

In the 17th century, the British bourgeoisie gradually came into power. The capitalistic economy was a prerequisite of the industrial revolution in the United Kingdom. The steam engine, invented by James Watt in the 18th century, was the icon of the technological revolution and globalization during the Anglo-American era. The introduction of the Watt steam engine provided an effective universal engine for industry, particularly the transportation industry, thereby promoting the industrial revolution in the United Kingdom.

The United Kingdom expanded the British Empire, establishing colonies in foreign lands and accelerating the accumulation of resources. British industrial production increased concurrently with colonial expansion, promoting globalization and establishing global markets. Classical economists developed the first theories of economic globalization during this period to assert its reasonableness and legitimacy. The economist Adam Smith developed a systematic theoretical logic to explain the strong expansion characteristics of market economy development. Smith explained that people innately desire to interact with one another and pursue wealth, thereby promoting the division of labor and market expansion, improving economic effectiveness, increasing economic output and national wealth, and promoting social development. Smith emphasized that a market economy based on exchange is dependent on promoting the professional division of labor and market expansion. The promotion of labor division and market expansion inevitably spread globally through exchanges.

The globalization of the British Empire was bloody and achieved through conquest and colonization. The driving force of this expansion was economic prosperity. To the United Kingdom, foreign lands denoted not only new territory but also new trade routes, market shares, and financial markets. The United Kingdom valued free trade to preserve these markets and its own interests.

Globalization led by the United Kingdom was quickly met by anti-globalization movements. Because of the predatory characteristics of capital, inequality associated with capital power quickly spread across the world. Class, nationality, race, and gender became the major reasons for anti-globalization protests. Adam Smith once expressed strong disapproval of the United Kingdom's exploitation of Bengal. He stated that the British destroyed Bengal's agricultural economy by plundering land that people used to grow food to establish poppy plantations, thereby effectively exacerbating the food shortage situation in Bengal into a state of famine, all so that the United Kingdom could export opium to China. This form of exploitation eventually caused large-scale famine in Bengal. The United Kingdom also desired control over India's manufacturing industry. India produced high-quality cotton and the country was able to maintain competitiveness even though its production systems were outdated compared with those of the United Kingdom. During the early 1700s, the United Kingdom introduced strict tariffs to quash India's competitiveness.

Early unilateral free trade policy of the United Kingdom

The industrial revolution of the United Kingdom involved many wealthy merchants, noble landlords, and wealthy handicraftsmen, all of whom invested in factories. New industrial cities emerged, enabling the industrial bourgeoisie population to increase in size and power. However, British landlords and noblemen strove to preserve old tariff systems such as the Corn Laws, which opposed the free trading of corn. The 19th century was an era of opposition among new free trade systems, which benefited the industrial bourgeoisie, and old tariff systems, which benefited noble land-lords. This struggle centered on the conflict between the preservation or abolition of the Corn Laws. The United Kingdom's then prime minister, Robert Peel, repealed the Corn Laws and promoted free trade thinking. In 1846, Peel argued the following in Parliament in defense of a unilateral free trade policy:

> If other countries choose to buy in the dearest market, such an option on their part constitutes no reason why we should not be permitted to buy in the cheapest. I trust the Government . . . will not resume the policy which they and we have found most inconvenient, namely, the haggling with foreign countries about reciprocal concessions, instead of taking that independent course which we believe to be conducive to our own interests. Let us trust to the influence of public opinion in other countries – let us trust that our example, with the proof of practical benefits we derive from it, will at no remote period insure the adoption of the principles on which we have acted.
>
> (Bhagwati, 2010)

Peel's argument is evidence that the free trade advocated by the emerging British bourgeoisie was unilateral.

Why was free trade unilateral? Many countries had yet to see the benefits of free trade or form free trade ideologies in the 19th century. The free trade system created by the United Kingdom was unilateral and bilateral. Unilateral free trade refers to the United Kingdom remaining committed to free trade regardless of whether the trading country accepted free trade. By contrast, bilateral free trade refers to reciprocal free trade. The United Kingdom believed that reciprocal tariff requests created problems for free trade merchants in other countries because such requests implied that free trade stood to benefit the United Kingdom rather than the merchants. Therefore, global governance ideologies of the time were centered on unilateral free trade, the United Kingdom did not emphasize reciprocity.

In the 20th century, particularly after the capitalistic economic crises in 1932, the economic and technological competitiveness of the United Kingdom regressed, forcing the British government to abandon its long-standing free trade policy and adopt policies to protect domestic trade, announcing that an ad valorem tax would be imposed on all foreign goods entering British markets. To preserve economic relations between the United Kingdom and its self-governing territories and colonies, an imperial preference system similar to a customs union was established between the British government and its self-governing territories and colonies.

Globalization during American imperialism

Early trade governance ideologies of the United States of America

Influenced by Adam Smith's *The Wealth of Nations*, the first US Secretary of State, Thomas Jefferson, advocated free trade and opposed high tariffs. Jefferson's political stance reflected the economic reality and stakes of domestic interest groups during the early development of the United States. During this period, agriculture was at the core of the American economy. The US government advocated free trade because plantation owners and farmers relied heavily on foreign, particularly European, markets. The views of the Democratic-Republican Party formed by Jefferson reflected the interests of northern business groups. Northern merchants actively engaged in trade with foreign merchants. The American manufacturing industry and its interest groups were still relatively weak during this period, and thus did not influence the formulation of American trade policies.

Alexander Hamilton, the first Secretary of the Treasury, held opposing views to those of Jefferson. In the *Report of Manufactures* presented to Congress in December 1791, Hamilton advocated considerable tariff increases and restrictions on importing foreign goods. He believed that this was the only method to stimulate the development of domestic industries and achieve economic independence. In Hamilton's opinion, if the United States, which primarily produced agricultural products at the time, opposed the development of the manufacturing industry, the country would gradually shift from a manufacturing economy to an agricultural one. The American trade policy makers emerged based on the Hamiltonian economic program, advocating trade protectionism and calling on the manufacturing industry to fortify the country. Trade protectionism gradually became the mainstream trade governance ideology during the initial developmental years of the United States.

The American industrial system was established under trade protection, with productivity surpassing that of the United Kingdom in or around 1897. After World War I, the United States replaced the United Kingdom as the world's largest economy. Thereafter, the United Kingdom repealed its free trade policy, imposing "McKenna Duties" on imported goods in 1915 and passing several tariff laws by 1932. Around the same time, the United States began its free trade period. In 1932, the Roosevelt administration replaced the Hoover administration, which supported low taxes and high tariffs. The

Roosevelt administration created the conditions that later facilitated free trade, passing the Reciprocal Trade Agreements Act in 1934, thereby marking the transition of trade protectionism to trade liberalism in the United States.

Globalization led by the United States

The United Kingdom became the world's largest economy during the first industrial revolution thanks to the invention of the steam engine. The American and German manufacturing industries flourished during the second industrial revolution, which was centered on the reform of electrical and petroleum technologies. The main classic capitalist production model during the second industrial revolution was the Fordist production system. Fordism was successfully implemented and promoted in the United States and subsequently spread globally. This production system restored the world economy, which was on the brink of collapse in the 1930s, and promoted the globalization of production, international trade, and finance. Fordism popularized the first wave of US-led globalization; Fordist globalization fueled corporate capitalism and formed a single global market. During this period, the United States gained control over global governance and established international rules based on a multilateral system to manage the processes of the single global market.

The underlying defects of Fordism began to emerge in the 1970s. The extreme hierarchical division of labor within enterprise organizations created motivational issues, making it extremely difficult to enhance labor productivity through the scientification of labor processes. Amidst increasing market saturation and consumption diversification, production methods centered on producing long-term standardized products no longer had mass production benefits, and enterprise organization under Fordism was no longer able to yield high profits.

With the dilemma of Fordism, neoliberalism became popular in the 1970s, catalyzed by Thatcherism in the United Kingdom and Reaganism in the United States. The global production paradigm shifted from the single-country manufacturing ideology of Fordism to multi-country manufacturing, consequently forming global value chains.

Global value chains are global, cross-enterprise network organizations that link production, sales, and recycling processes to realize the value of products and services. These chains sequentially involve the collection and transportation of raw materials, manufacturing and distribution of semi-finished and finished products, and finally the consumption and recycling of these products. These chains encompass all participants and organizations involved in the production and sales processes, as well as their value and profit distribution. A number of scholars have used the term "fragmentation" to describe the segmentation of the production process, arguing that this type of production process is a recent phenomenon in global separation. This separation, coined "the new unbundling" by American economist Richard Baldwin, is a key phenomenon in cross-industrial production organizations, and reflects the multinational potential of capital.

From the perspective of global trade governance, the United States' current stage of globalization implies new challenges, particularly the challenge of the "governance gap" in the global economy. The multilateral trade system that emerged after World War II facilitated the first wave of US-led globalization, opening a world market for international trade among developed countries. The second wave of US-led globalization was driven by finance and investments, thereby changing the scope of global production. The current multilateral trade system regulated by the WTO cannot cope with the new, ever-changing global economic environment, or "new unbundling" environment, as characterized by Richard Baldwin. Therefore, as the regulating body for global trade governance, the WTO is in a state of confusion, unable to form new governance mechanisms and regulations.

Trade governance ideology of the United States

During the Cold War, the international strategy adopted by the United States was to boycott the Soviet Union and strengthen ties with China. The global trade governance ideology of the United States was the implementation of the GATT to transform the free trade system into a tool for use during the Cold War. The United States aimed to establish a free trade system to revive the economies of its key allies, namely Western Europe and Japan, and collectively boycott the Soviet Union. In contrast to the policy of the Soviet Union, President Nixon reached out to China in the 1970s. Subsequently, China applied to join the GATT in the mid-1980s, expressing interest in being part of the global trade system. For the United States, multilateralism was a tool of self-interest. The country adopted a multilateral framework to realize the interests of specific countries rather than the collective interests of every member in the system. The United States was simultaneously the primary driving force of and largest obstruction to multilateral cooperation. This paradox is a principal characteristic of the United States' participation in global trade governance.

The global trade governance of the United States became increasingly reliant on regionalism at the beginning of the 1990s, marked by the ratification of the North American Free Trade Agreement (NAFTA). The United States implemented a free trade agreement (FTA) strategy during this period. This transition to a strategy to erode the multilateral system became increasingly evident after the attacks of 11 September 2001 (hereinafter

9/11). Between the George W. Bush and Barack Obama administrations, the United States achieved substantial progress in terms of its implementation of the Free Trade Zone (FTZ) strategy. The period during which the United States replaced its multilateral system with regional and bilateral agreements can be characterized into three distinct stages, detailed as follows.

The first stage was the introduction of the "participation and expansion" foreign policy, initially proposed by the Clinton administration, which valued regional economic cooperation. In the Third Ministerial Conference of the WTO held in Seattle in 1999, the delegates failed to agree on the agenda. To some extent, the lack of consensus weakened the United States' prominent status in the multilateral system, initiating the country's gradual shift toward regional governance.

The second stage was the period during which the Bush administration attempted to establish a post-Westphalia system in 2001, after 9/11. The government attempted to achieve unipolar hegemony with the United States at the center. Because most of the terrorists at that time originated from the Middle East, this region naturally became the focus of American diplomacy efforts, prioritizing the establishment of an FTA with Middle Eastern countries. Before 9/11, the only Middle Eastern country that had an FTA with the United States was Israel. In 2003, the Bush administration proposed the United States Middle East Free Trade Area.

Delegates failed to reach a consensus for a second time at the Fifth Ministerial Conference of the WTO held in Cancun, Mexico, in 2003. This failure essentially led to the collapse of the multilateral system and accelerated bilateral negotiations between the United States and other countries. The United States sequentially signed FTAs with Chile, Peru, Colombia, Mexico, Canada, the Dominican Republic, Costa Rica, South Korea, and Australia.

The third stage of the United States replacing its multilateral system with regional and bilateral agreements was the introduction of the regionalism agenda proposed by the Obama administration. After the outbreak of the 2007–2008 financial crisis, the Obama administration proposed a reindustrialization strategy in an attempt to expand exports. Because of the stagnation of the Doha Development Round, the United States was unable to expand the scope of its manufacturing exports through multilateral trade arrangements, and thus introduced a mega cross-regional trade negotiation approach to initiate TPP negotiations. The United States and Europe formally announced the Transatlantic Trade and Investment Partnership (TTIP) negotiations during the G8 Summit in June 2013. As world economic powers, developed countries such as the United States and Western European countries initiated a new round of global economic integration. The TPP and TTIP became key globalization strategies of the United States.

Recession of Anglo-Saxon globalization

Under many circumstances, "anti-globalization" is a general and abstract term. The formulation of anti-globalization is similar to those of "anti-neoliberalism," "anti-capitalism," "anti-global economy," "anti-free trade," "anti-(capitalist) systems," "anti-Americanism," "anti-hegemonism," and "anti-multinational corporations."

I attended the WTO Ministerial Conferences in Seattle in 1999, Doha in 2001, Mexico in 2003, and Hong Kong in 2005. During these conferences, I witnessed anti-globalization activists adopt numerous aggressive and nonviolent measures to voice their opposition. Some activists sat outside the venue in silent protest while the conference was conducted; others participated in public rallies involving opposition speeches. Some even put themselves at risk by engaging in violent riots. Generally, anti-globalization protests have grown increasingly aggressive. These incidents are just snippets of anti-globalization movements.

In 2016, two major political events occurred: the United Kingdom's decision to leave the European Union and the election of Donald Trump as president of the United States. Both events occurred in developed Western countries at a time when the United Kingdom and the United States were leaders of globalization. These events profoundly subverted globalization, causing a regression in the Anglo-Saxon style of liberal British and American civilizations. The United Kingdom and United States are countries with distinct identities; the United States calls itself the "City on the Hill," and the United Kingdom distances itself from mainland Europe. These countries had previously dominated globalization and gained control of global trade governance, simultaneously promoting American Exceptionalism and Pax Americana.

Brexit and the election of Trump imply the recession of the global governance system. Brexit symbolizes the recession of European integration, casting doubt on the future of European integration and consequently weakening the political cohesion of the European Union. The election of Trump symbolizes the imminent collapse of the US-regulated multilateral trade system. The Trump administration intends to renegotiate NAFTA, has suspended TPP negotiations with Asia-Pacific countries, and is vigorously promoting trade protectionism. These efforts not only imply that current multilateral or global system frameworks are poised to undergo changes but also indicate that the core element of global governance, namely regulations, are no longer respected. Brexit and the election of Trump represent the greatest recession in global governance since World War II.

China proposed the B&R amidst the recession of globalization and global trade governance. China's historical background raises the question of how the relationship between the B&R and globalization should be viewed.

First, policies must drive development and progress among the entire human race to become an inevitable trend and must achieve globalization that is objective and facilitates steady historical development. China's B&R conforms to the laws of historical development and evolution. Furthermore, the origin of the problems due to globalization led by the United Kingdom and United States must be analyzed to facilitate the development of a new era of globalization and global governance. Trump's solution is to accept reverse globalization and ignore existing local trade governance protocols to ensure his "America First" policy. What China advocates and how we can elucidate the trade governance ideologies of the B&R require further investigation.

3 Economic logic of the B&R

China's participation in the process of globalization and proposal of the B&R

Although China initiated globalization during the agriculture-pasturing period, the country missed a historic opportunity to be recognized as the forerunner of globalization. Specifically, the treasure voyages by Zheng He during the Ming dynasty occurred earlier than the voyages of Columbus and were conducted on a greater scale, thereby highlighting China's technological achievements. However, it was Europe that gained historical recognition for discovering the "New World" and promoting the industrial revolution and formation of the global market.

After World War II, China was initially based on a planned economy because the government was unfamiliar with the concept of a global economy. The recent integration of China into globalization can be classified into three stages. The first stage was the period between 1978 and 2000, the general feature of which was China's partial participation in globalization and opening up to the world amidst the advancement of domestic economic reform. In 1986, China applied to join the General Agreement on Tariffs and Trade (GATT) and gradually improved domestic trade legislation through the advancement of GATT negotiations. The second stage spanned from 2001 to 2008, the general feature of which was China's shift to complete participation in globalization. China joined the World Trade Organization (WTO) in 2001, marking its integration into a multilateral system and the beginning of its involvement in global governance. Facilitated by the openness of the multilateral trade system, China's economy grew exponentially. The third stage is the current period from 2008 onward, the general feature of which is China's full involvement in globalization. China led governance and remediation movements following the outbreak of the global financial crisis. In September 2013, China proposed the B&R, bringing the world into a new stage of global governance. "B&R" refers to the Silk Road

Economic Belt and the 21st Century Maritime Silk Road. The initiative aims to fully utilize existing bilateral and multilateral mechanisms between China and countries along the B&R routes, existent and effective regional cooperation platforms, and the historical reputation of the ancient Silk Road to promote fair development, actively encourage economic partnerships with coastal countries, and cocreate a politically accepting, economically integrated, and culturally accepting community of shared interests, destiny, and responsibility.

Currently, over 100 countries and international organizations are participating in the realization of the B&R. China has already signed cooperation agreements with over 30 coastal countries and international industrial capacity cooperation agreements with over 20 countries. International organizations such as the United Nations (UN) have also expressed interest in expanding financial cooperation through the Asian Infrastructure Investment Bank and Silk Road Fund to gradually assist the formation of a number of key influential projects.

Opportunities for developing countries to establish global value chains

In recent years, the formation and development of global value chains have drastically changed the production paradigms. Global value chains are embodied by the internationalization of production processes and international distribution of products, investments, services, knowledge, and people. Global value chains strengthen ties and interests between countries. Although opposition to globalization exists, globalization neither ceases nor regresses.

The B&R is the largest regional cooperation initiative to date, encompassing Asia, Europe, and Africa, opening to the rest of the world. At one end is the active East Asian economic circle, and at the other is the developed European economic circle, collectively involving over 60 countries, 60% of the global population, and a third of the world's gross domestic product (GDP).

Substantial heterogeneity exists in the economic development of the coastal countries involved in the B&R because of the geographical scope of the initiative and situations in different countries. Regarding income, Central and Eastern European countries have high average incomes. By contrast, the average incomes in approximately 70% of all other countries involved in the B&R are below the global average. From the perspective of income growth rate per capita, the regions covered by the B&R exhibit rapidly increasing overall growth rates, with over 75 of these countries over the global average. In particular, the income growth rate per capita in Central,

Eastern, and Southern Asian countries is higher than that in the other countries involved. Overall, average income varies considerably among all countries involved in the B&R, most of which are developing countries. Most of the countries with high average incomes are resource-based countries that lack the incentive to promote overall regional development.

Most countries along the B&R routes involved in the B&R are developing countries. A large portion of these countries do not enjoy a share of the benefits of globalization and are in dire need of joining a global value chain. China gained the opportunity to join global value chains after being accepted into the WTO. The Chinese manufacturing industry typically provides original equipment manufacturing in global value chains, and thus sits at the lower ends of chains. However, globalization has provided an opportunity for China to participate in the international division of labor, enabling a portion of the industry to gradually ascend the value chains and become increasingly competitive. Whether China can assist developing countries in joining value chains through the incentives provided by the B&R remains to be seen.

Globalization has enabled developing countries to join global value chains and acquire technologies to enhance their industrial development and factor endowments. A number of emerging and developing countries are capable of becoming leaders in the reconstruction of value chains. Value chains based in developing countries have the following features.

First, value chains based in developing countries can gradually achieve the effective allocation of resources only in specific regions because of limited capital size, technical capabilities, and system quality. These chains are not yet able to drive global production networks. Therefore, value chains based in developing countries exhibit regional characteristics.

Second, value chains based in developing countries are based on the industries essential for industrialization in such countries and industries with technical advantages in emerging countries. The more developed and prominent industries in global value chains are the automobile and electronics industries, the main features of which are (1) that the two ends of the smile curve are controlled by developed countries and their enterprises; (2) that although the division of labor within these industries is complex, their technical specifications are unified and they have established modular production systems; and (3) that they are part of long value chains comprising many enterprises. Developing countries cannot compete in developed global value chains. Alternatively, they can choose to promote industries that are involved in shorter value chains, such as the apparel or food industries. Technical decomposition and spatial separability (e.g., modulation) exist in the various production stages of developed value chains. Therefore, developing countries can create regional value chains based around industries with relatively easier production processes.

Third, a common objective of developing countries is to enhance industrialization and promote economic development. A previous study indicated that the time of employing import substitution strategies to realize industrialization has passed. The reason is simple: countries that adopt import substitution strategies may avoid national trade, causing domestic production systems to close down. The emergence and development of regional value chains provides developing countries with new opportunities for industrialization and economic growth. By participating in regional value chains, countries become involved in international trade and join industrial networks, thereby creating and improving domestic production systems.

Fourth, the purpose of value chains based in developing countries is to promote development. Currently, global value chains distribute interest unevenly; the smile curves shift from fairly flat (interest is distributed evenly along the value chain) to U-shaped (uneven distribution of interest). According to the aforementioned second feature, developing countries that seek opportunities to establish value chains based around industries involved in relatively short value chains can prevent the rapid formation of U-shaped value chains, thereby guaranteeing even distribution of interest over a specific period to achieve mutual development objectives.

Fifth, the establishment of regional value chains led by developing countries generates a new policy spillover effect. Governments have a substantial influence on industry policies and countries within the region in question. Policy cooperation content no longer centers on aspects of traditional FTAs such as tariff barriers but rather focuses on trade and investment policy integration based on value chain theory.

Since China's introduction of the B&R, various projects have been launched involving the energy, infrastructure, and agriculture industries. These industries highlight the factor endowment competitiveness and industrialization potential of developing countries. The greatest appeal of the B&R to developing countries is opportunities to establish regional production networks and resolving the challenges of mutual development through project connectivity.

Possibility of establishing a B&R regional industrial chain: China and the Eurasia Economic Union as an example

Statuses of China and B&R coastal countries in global value chains

Koopman et al. proposed the GVC Participation Index to calculate the international division of labor status in a specific industry of a specific country in its global value chain. Specifically, the index compares the intermediate export volume of the industry (intermediate goods into a foreign country to produce and export finished goods) with the intermediate import volume of the same industry in the host country (intermediate goods into the host county to produce and export finished goods). The equation can be expressed as follows:

$$GVC\_Positon_{ir} = \ln(1 + IV_{ir} / E_{ir}) - (1 + FV_{ir} / E_{ir})$$

where $GVC\_Positon_{ir}$ represents the status of the international division of labor in the ith industry of the rth country in its global value chain, and IV_{ir} represents the indirect value-added exports of the ith industry of the rth country or the trade volume of intermediate goods exported by the ith industry of the rth country. The index measures the amount of added value in the intermediate exports of the ith industry of the rth country that is processed by another country and exported to a third country. In addition, FV_{ir} represents the overseas value-added exports of the ith industry of the rth country or the value of intermediate goods imported from a foreign country contained in the finished goods exported by the ith industry of the rth country. E_{ir} represents the export value of the ith industry of the rth country calculated based on "added value." The equation shows that when the amount of indirect value-added exports (IV_{ir}) is higher than that of overseas value-added exports (FV_{ir}) in overall exports (E_{ir}), the GVC Participation Index is greater than zero. Enterprises that are higher in the global value chain play a more prominent role in the chain, whereas those lower in the chain have a less prominent status.

Koopman's GVC Participation Index was adopted in this book to calculate the division of labor in B&R coastal countries in their global value chains (Table 3.1).[1]

Table 3.1 shows that China's overall GVC Participation Index increased annually in the period in question, reaching 0.038 in 2008. Thereafter, the index decreased slightly but was maintained at 0.029 in 2011, evidencing

Table 3.1 Total GVC Participation Indices

	1995	2000	2005	2008	2009	2010	2011
China	−0.01351	−0.05967	−0.04022	0.038038	0.034651	0.026314	0.029313
Russia	0.362141	0.337884	0.425651	0.402223	0.406735	0.406155	0.399981
24 Coastal Countries	0.162061	0.098371	0.115118	0.123876	0.127747	0.123474	0.126778

Source: OECD-WTO TiVA Total Exports Decomposition Table; GVC Participation Indices were calculated by the author

the participation of China in global value chains during this period. The GVC Participation Indices of the 24 coastal countries were relatively high, implying that the Association of Southeast Asian Nations (ASEAN) and Central and Eastern European countries were deeply involved in regional value chains. Russia had the highest GVC Participation Index, suggesting that it had a high proportion of high added-value resource industries in its export structure. Countries with low value-added exports can focus on developing resource industries that are involved in shorter value chains.

Connectivity between China and the Eurasia Economic Union

China should establish B&R regional value chains within specific geographical ranges and in institutional regions. In this book, we selected Eurasia Economic Union (EAEU) countries as targets for a probability analysis. The EAEU is an organization centered on regional economic integration. It was founded on 1 January 2015 under the collective efforts of Russia, Belarus, and Kazakhstan. The organization focuses on promoting the free flow of products, services, capital, and labor among countries. On 2 January 2015, Armenia became the fourth EAEU country, and Kyrgyzstan became the fifth in August of the same year. The EAEU's free trade agreement (FTA) negotiations with China have ended. The outcomes constitute a possible system guarantee for the establishment of a value chain.

The EAEU is a classic integrated organization. A large number of B&R construction projects are investment projects; however, the real focus should be the establishment of regional value chains. "One Belt One League" connectivity should not only consider the FTA negotiation model of the EAEU but also explore the possibilities of establishing regional value chains.

First, China has the potential to establish regional value chains based on leading industries in specific regions. The Hungarian economist Balassa introduced revealed comparative advantage indices (RCA indices) to quantify and describe the export performance of various product-related industries in a country and uncover the international trade competitiveness of the country. An RCA index refers to the ratio of the export volume of a specific product in the overall national export volume to that in the global export volume. The equation can be expressed as follows:

$$RCA_{ij} = \frac{\left(X_{ij} \middle/ \sum_{i=1}^{n} X_{ij} \right)}{\left(\sum_{j=1}^{m} X_{ij} \middle/ \sum_{j=1}^{m} \sum_{i=1}^{n} X_{ij} \right)}$$

where X_{ij} represents the export value of the *i*th product in the *j*th country.

Generally, an RCA value that approximates 1 denotes neutral comparative advantage or no relative advantage or disadvantage. An RCA value greater than 1 denotes that the national export ratio of a product is greater than the global export ratio of the product. This situation denotes that the product is competitive in the international market. An RCA value lower than 1 denotes that the product is not competitive in the international market. The competitiveness of various Chinese industries classified using the Harmonized System (HS) is tabulated in Table 3.2.

Table 3.2 shows that the most competitive industries were raw hides and skins, leather, furskins, and articles thereof; saddles and harnesses; travel goods; textiles and textile products; footwear; and headgear. These industries all achieved RCA values of over 2.5. Other highly competitive industries were stone and articles of stone; ceramic products; glass; machinery, mechanical equipment, electrical equipment, and parts thereof; and television image and sound recorders and reproducers. The moderately competitive industries were plastics and articles thereof, rubber and articles thereof, and wood and articles thereof; wood charcoal; base metals and articles thereof; and optical, photographic, cinematographic, measuring, checking, medical, and surgical instruments and apparatus and precision instruments and equipment. These data show that the competitive industries of China were mainly traditional manufacturing industries. These industries have simple manufacturing processes and technical modules and short value chains. They are consistent with the feasible industries for establishing regional value chains in developing countries categorized in this book. These industries will inevitably serve as the dominant force in the connectivity of the B&R.

Second, China has a dominant comparative advantage over EAEU countries. In addition to measuring industrial competitiveness, RCA indices can be used to determine the comparative advantage of a region. The following equation was used to calculate the comparative advantage indices of China and other regions:

$$RCA = \frac{China's\ Exports\ to\ a\ Specific\ Region\ /\ China's\ Total\ Exports}{World\ Exports\ to\ a\ Specific\ Region\ /\ Total\ Global\ Exports}$$

Table 3.3 shows that China is highly competitive with Kyrgyzstan and Kazakhstan. In particular, the RCA index of China to Kyrgyzstan in 2008 was 25, steadily reducing to approximately 4.4 in 2015. Moreover, China is moderately competitive with Russia and exhibits weak competitiveness with the remaining two countries.

Table 3.2 RCA indices of Chinese industries

RCA	2010	2011	2012	2013	2014	2015
Live Animals; Animal Products	0.4176	0.4362	0.4253	0.4040	0.4006	0.3892
Vegetable Products	0.4201	0.3980	0.3413	0.3490	0.3425	0.3557
Animal or Vegetable Fats and Oils and Their Cleavage Products; Prepared Edible Fats; Animal or Vegetable Waxes	0.0434	0.0467	0.0479	0.0542	0.0538	0.0559
Prepared Foodstuffs; Beverages, Spirits and Vinegar; Tobacco and Manufactured Tobacco Substitutes	0.4192	0.4457	0.4559	0.4182	0.4011	0.3799
Mineral Products	0.1134	0.0975	0.8616	0.9022	0.0940	0.1103
Products of the Chemical or Allied Industries	0.5171	0.5830	0.5386	0.5164	0.5395	0.5102
Plastics and Articles Thereof; Rubber and Articles Thereof	0.7251	0.7936	0.8783	0.8953	0.8947	0.8572
Raw Hides and Skins, Leather, Furskins, and Articles Thereof; Saddlery and Harnesses; Travel Goods, Handbags, and Similar Containers; Articles of Animal Gut (other than Silkworm Gut)	2.4563	2.6211	2.5257	2.3789	2.2591	2.1536
Wood and Articles Thereof; Wood Charcoal; Cork and Articles Thereof; Products of Straw, Esparto, and Other Plaiting Materials; Basketware and Wickerwork	0.9680	1.0023	1.0295	0.9005	0.8939	0.8691
Pulp of Wood or Other Fibrous Cellulosic Material; Recovered (Waste and Scrap) Paper or Paperboard; Paper and Paperboard and Articles Thereof	0.4551	0.5336	0.6055	0.6359	0.6511	0.6740
Textiles and Textile Articles	2.9582	3.0232	2.9680	2.9135	2.7838	2.5125
Footwear, Headgear, Umbrellas, Parasols, Walking Sticks, Seat Sticks, Whips, Riding Crops, and Parts Thereof; Prepared Feathers and Articles Made Therewith; Artificial Flowers; Articles of Human Hair	3.7955	3.8098	3.9102	3.6927	3.4987	3.0602
Articles of Stone, Plaster, Cement, Asbestos, Mica, and Similar Materials; Ceramic Products; Glass and Glassware	1.8530	2.0143	2.1726	2.2083	2.1698	2.2660
Natural or Cultured Pearls, Precious or Semiprecious Stones, Precious Metals, Metals Clad with Precious Metals, and Articles Thereof; Imitation Jewelry; Coins	0.2735	0.4128	0.5224	0.4963	0.7060	0.3451

Base Metals and Articles Thereof	0.9506	1.0288	1.0616	1.0783	1.1668	1.1616
Machinery and Mechanical Appliances, Electrical Equipment, and Parts Thereof; Sound Recorders and Reproducers, Television Image and Sound Recorders and Reproducers and Parts and Accessories of Such Articles	1.7750	1.8153	1.8288	1.8350	1.7320	1.6227
Vehicles, Aircrafts, Vessels, and Associated Transport Equipment	0.5602	0.5910	0.5403	0.4610	0.4450	0.4650
Optical, Photographic, Cinematographic, Measuring, Medical, and Surgical Instruments and Apparatus; Clocks and Watches; Musical Instruments; Parts and Accessories of the Above	1.0421	1.0750	1.1629	1.1192	1.0250	0.9686
Arms and Ammunition; Parts and Accessories Thereof	0.0737	0.0786	0.0781	0.0734	0.0906	0.0680
Miscellaneous Manufactured Articles	3.0388	3.1573	3.2826	3.1778	3.0580	2.9379
Works of Art, Collectors' Items, and Antiques	0.0865	0.1763	0.2036	0.3588	0.1736	0.1004
Special Trade Articles and Unclassified Articles	0.0459	0.0712	0.0364	0.0451	0.0493	0.0619

Source: UN Comtrade Database; HS for Classification

Table 3.3 Dominant comparative advantages of China and other EAEU countries

	2007	2008	2009	2010	2011	2012	2013	2014	2015
Belarus	0.0894	0.1024	0.1006	0.2177	0.1468	0.1776	0.1730	0.2208	0.1783
Russia	1.6128	1.3827	1.0506	1.2347	1.2104	1.2482	1.3440	1.5080	1.3607
Kyrgyzstan	17.1220	25.2541	18.0123	12.2243	10.9042	8.4586	7.2407	4.3991	4.4821
Kazakhstan	2.5718	2.9004	2.7945	3.7029	2.3970	2.2128	2.1941	2.4791	3.0980
Armenia	0.1902	0.1884	0.2822	0.2956	0.3145	0.2377	0.2404	0.2376	0.2492

Source: UN Comtrade Database

Third, the EAEU requires trade and investment facilitation and industrialization. Armenia, Kazakhstan, Kyrgyzstan, and Belarus had low degrees of trade facilitation. EAEU countries are located inland and lack infrastructure. These factors influence their ability to facilitate trade and increase trade costs. The import time of Kazakhstan is typically 79 days and the import cost of Kyrgyzstan may be as high as US$6,000/box. EAEU countries are non-central in global value chains and are often excluded from them. Therefore, EAEU-B&R connectivity and infrastructure connectivity are primary objectives of the B&R to guarantee the provision of hardware to reinforce the trade facilitation efforts of EAEU countries. The B&R focuses on a number of industries to establish regional industrial chains and accelerate the industrialization of EAEU countries. Therefore, satisfying the requirements of EAEU countries enables the establishment of regional value chains.

Based on the preceding analysis, we deduced that the connectivity between China's B&R and the EAEU is a starting point for the establishment of regional value chains. First, investments in the consumer goods industries (e.g., apparel, leather, footwear, and headgear) of the EAEU countries should be increased to enhance the local production of consumer goods, satisfy basic domestic consumption requirements, and initiate the development of local industries. Second, investments in the chemical, infrastructure, and advanced material processing industries should be expanded. These industries serve as intermediaries connecting other industries and extend value chains. Expanding investments in these industries facilitate the exports of the machinery, mechanical equipment, and electrical appliance industries in China, thereby forming a linkage effect between investment and exports. Third, emerging industries such as the electronic and information industry should be promoted. The electronic and information industry is key to the establishment of global value chains. China has a technical advantage in promoting these industries to form regional value chains and encouraging EAEU countries to participate in these chains.

Win–win for the industrialization of China and developing countries

Industrialization is key to economic growth in developing countries. The American economist Hollis B. Chenery classified industrialization in developing countries into three stages. The first stage is the agricultural economy stage. The second is the industrialization stage, which is subcategorized into early, mid-, and late industrialization. The third stage is the developed economy stage. Chenery believed that differences between national trade strategies and policies stem from varying levels of industrialization of developing countries.

I traveled to Kazakhstan in 2016 to research the B&R and visit Chinese and local enterprises. Kazakhstan has an abundance of agricultural and mineral resources but correspondingly weak industries. Investments for the processing of agricultural goods provided by Chinese enterprises enable local industries to turn a profit (e.g., processing tomatoes into ketchup). Kazakhstan seemed uninterested in China's initial proposal of the B&R, maintaining a skeptical view on China's intentions. However, when China renegotiated the B&R with Kazakhstan from the perspective of industrialization, the initiative gained popularity among the local government and enterprises. After concluding my research in Kazakhstan and returning to China, I conducted a feasibility analysis on a number of EAEU countries. The analysis findings were consistent with my field survey; the B&R should aim to establish regional value chains to promote industrialization in developing countries. The factor endowments, industrial advantages, and investment capability of China meet the requirements of the B&R coastal countries. Therefore, consolidating B&R investments into regional value chains fits market criteria. Developing countries are in the initial stages of industrialization and require investments in light industry and infrastructure, which are advantageous for China. For example, industrialization and urbanization are the main objectives of India's economic growth policy. To achieve these objectives, India must expand its infrastructure and investments and accelerate construction within a short period. Chinese enterprises have gained the favor of the Indian government for tenders of construction undertakings. Establishing B&R value chains promotes globalization at a more reasonable level, benefits the rebalancing of globalization, absolves the conflict caused by globalization, and provides developing countries with opportunities for economic development. B&R strategies based on the establishment of value chains create mutually beneficial situations for China and coastal countries involved in the B&R.

Note

1 The B&R involves 65 countries and regions. The TiVa Database of the Organisation for Economic Co-operation and Development (OECD) and WTO was used to collect the samples of 25 ASEAN, South Asian, West Asian, and Central and Eastern European countries, including Singapore, Malaysia, Indonesia, Thailand, Cambodia, Vietnam, Brunei, the Philippines, India, Turkey, Israel, Saudi Arabia, Greece, Cyprus, Poland, Estonia, the Czech Republic, Slovakia, Hungary, Slovenia, and Romania. In addition, Russia was selected as an independent sample.

4 Value choices of B&R trade governance

Value of global governance

The gradual regression of the Anglo-Saxon style of globalization in 2016 and the announcement of the Unites States' withdrawal from the Trans-Pacific Partnership (TPP) by President Trump in 2017 highlighted that the multilateral trade system has entered a state of instability and various countries and people of different socioeconomic statuses are in a state of value disagreement. These situations cannot be explained simply from the perspective of trade; explanations based on value must be identified. Existing global trade systems have established a robust framework of WTO rules and basic principles based on the concept of the "most favored nation." Moreover, the regulations of global trade are based on the General Agreement on Trade in Goods, General Agreement on Trade in Services, and Agreement on Trade-Related Aspects of Intellectual Property Rights. Why can World Trade Organization (WTO) rules not save the current trade system? We believe this system lacks spirit and basic value consensus.

Basic value consensus refers to the consistency of problems or views. In a trade system, fair interactions and dialogues between WTO members must be established to achieve this type of consensus. In actuality, the negotiation, reform, and development of WTO rules constitute the continuous formation of value consensus, which is a continuous and uninterrupted process of demonstration, validation, and correction.

Economists and jurists have conflicting views on the value of policies and laws concerning global governance. Popular opinion is that policies and laws should be formulated based on "value neutrality" principles. Economists believe that economics is essentially the study of the effects of environmental changes on specific events, and thus involves prediction and analysis and is not associated with value. The conclusions of this view generally relate to whether or not a specific objective can be achieved and if so, how it can be achieved. In a stricter sense, economists do not discuss the positive or negative effects of these objectives. These judgments exclude value from economics. Other scholars, particularly liberal scholars, believe that freedom leads to neutrality. Liberalism is synonymous with pluralism. The goal of liberalism is to show acceptance for a variety of diversities. In other words, liberalists deem that all values and concepts are of equal importance and freedom. Therefore, such scholars maintain a neutral perspective on value principles.

Regarding whether global governance and policies and laws are valuable, I believe that adopting a value neutrality perspective is unrealistic. Neutrality is one of many opinions. From the perspective of liberalism, neutrality is generally considered a type of orientation. Some even consider neutrality the closest orientation to the ideal state, which is "valueless" global governance; however, this state does not exist in the real world.

First, global governance participants, economists, policy formulators, and legislators are human, and all laws governing our world were established by humans. Therefore, these laws were inevitably created based on the preferences of specific interests or social groups. The values held by these groups undoubtedly affected their research directions, policies, and legislative preferences.

Second, variety in value judgments exists in markets. Friedman proposed the following notable example: to engage in a transaction, the values of the participants must be different. If Mr. A possesses Item X and Mr. B possesses Item Y, and both parties believe that Item X is better than Item Y, the exchange of Item X for Item Y does not occur. Only when Mr. A perceives Item Y to be more valuable than Item X and Mr. B perceives Item X to be more valuable than Item Y can a transaction occur because both parties believe that they are benefiting from said transaction (Friedman, 1987). This example explains that transactions are fundamentally the coordination of different values or the achievement of consensus in an inconsistent situation. In contrast to one-time transactions, where all pieces of Item X are exchanged for all pieces of Item Y and both items are divisible quantities that are transacted gradually, the transaction between Mr. A and Mr. B continues until a marginal point where the two parties perceive the remaining pieces of Items X and Y to be equally valuable. Based on this example, parties engage in exchange to acquire consistent perceptions concerning value.

Third, certain values must be coadaptive and interactive to form systems and their institutions (including policies and legislation). Values are not formed through the mandatory undertakings of legislators, policy formulators, philosophers, and economists; they are ideas that are formed naturally. When a person's values begin to influence other people, they become an integral part of the overall social system. When a country's values begin to influence other countries, they become an integral part of an international system. In this subtle interaction, "we simultaneously become the actor and the viewer, the observer and the observed, the teacher and the student" (Friedman, 1987).

Therefore, researching global trade governance without value analysis is unrealistic. Global trade systems are built on institutional arrangements that combine international norms with mainstream values.

Lack of value consensus in global trade governance

The existing WTO system lacks a definitive interpretation of basic value consensus. Many believe that the value consensus of the WTO is free trade. However, some contend that free trade is merely a means for economic development and an economical choice that lacks value guidance. Current anti-globalization campaigns have put liberalism on the inspection table. For the first time, people are doubting the viability of freedom as a universal value.

The lack of consensus concerning values in global systems is reflected by value differences and value conflict. Value differences are normal in global systems. The world is composed of a diverse spectrum of ethnicities and worldviews. Value conflict constitutes the "metamorphosis" of value differentiation, where conflict causes value differences to evolve into confrontation or opposition. At the other end of the spectrum, values may also converge; for example, neoliberalism reached its golden era in the 20th century. However, this state of "complete unification" is also one state of extreme tension that has the potential to unravel into crisis.

Global trade systems lack value consensus. The development of global trade systems is gradually shifting toward value conflict and exhibits historical inevitability.

First, globalization leads to the division of national production and hinders poor and wealthy countries from achieving value consensus. Two decades ago, UN members included only approximately 20 least developed countries. That number is now 48. Three billion people are living on less than US$2 per day, and 1.3 billion are living below the absolute poverty threshold of US$1 per day (Jiao, 2005).

Second, internal division has widened the poverty gap in some countries. The 1993 book *Manufacturing on the Move* by Robert Crandall, a member of the Brookings Institution, systematically described how Rust Belt manufacturing in the United States was gradually shifting overseas and to the southern and western regions of the country. The Rust Belt peaked in the 1950s, at one point accounting for as much as 45% of the United States' overall economy. During this period, over 50% of industrial workers worked in the Rust Belt and the unemployment rate declined annually.

These conditions gave rise to populism, anti-globalization, and doubts over literalism.

Third, the values of various countries that were once converged have begun to diverge again, rekindling the conflict between nationalism and civilizationism. Values of different countries always vary initially. Amidst globalization, these values have converged. In China, people's values have gradually transitioned from conservative to liberal values amidst reform and increasing openness. However, when a global crisis occurred, some people returned to populism; under such circumstances, people are likely to return to their original value systems in search of safety.

The preceding discussion explains that global trade systems currently lack value consensus and have entered a stage of regression. Therefore, from the perspective of global governance, regaining the values associated with global trade systems is critical.

Erroneous values

"Zero-sum game" values

A zero-sum game is a situation in which a participant's gain or loss of utility is exactly balanced by the utility losses or gains of the other participants. In other words, if the total gains of the participants are added up and the total losses are subtracted, the sum is zero. The "America First" foreign policy proposed by the Trump administration constitutes a "you or me" situation. The United States is the inventor of unfair trade, which in actuality is a concept built on self-interest. "Unfair" refers to inequality generated by foreign competition, for which a country must seek protection. The domestic trade legislation of the United States is based on this concept; Section 301 of the Trade Act authorizes the president to take all appropriate action, including retaliation, to remove any act, policy, or practice of a foreign government that violates an international trade agreement. However, this policy does not provide competitive countries or products fair market competition opportunities, but rather essentially restricts those that are competitive. The "America First" foreign policy clearly exhibits the US government's intention toward self-preservation. This policy is based on "you or me" values, where you are fair to me or I am fair to you, or you are unemployed or I am unemployed.

"Winner takes all" values

After World War II, the United States began to design a global governance system. The United States had the initiative in the international arena and attempted to promote its values through hegemony. In this hegemonic strategy, American values were prioritized. These values were metaphorically depicted as "the United States serves as the world police" or "the United States is on your face," and guaranteed power and profit for the United States. In this international system, "the United States takes all" and all other countries exist in harmony because of the United States.

"Win more lose less" values

Some American scholars have argued that the "winner takes all" design is unfair, and that the United States' preservation of its imperial status will one day be its downfall. This concept was coined the "backfire effect," where persistence is met with resistance. In the advantage strategy proposed by Professor Art, "advantage implies that a country wins more and loses less than other countries." "Win more lose less" values were proposed by the United States in relation to a realistic international environment.

"Mutual demise" values

"Mutual demise" values, otherwise referred to as the determination to lose, generally occur during periods of immense fluctuation in the global system.

The common trait of the "zero-sum game," "winner takes all," "win more lose less," and "mutual demise" values is that they are formed based on self-perceived judgments of value and interest. People naturally center value judgments on themselves; poor people believe that "wealth equality" is fair, whereas wealthy people believe that capital gains are justly deserved. These self-centric approaches to judging value lead to diametrical opposition.

Value choices of B&R trade governance

The targets of global trade governance are a global issue on a global scale. Value choices should fully encompass all concepts and ideas and differences between countries. These choices should aim to achieve sharing and the balance of interest within global systems. The value of B&R governance can be determined based on the following guidelines.

Holism

China deems events or systems as frameworks that contain opposition and symbiosis. All entities in a system have various possible interrelationships. China adopts a holistic worldview to assess the world, thereby forming a notable contrast with the "winner takes all" and "zero-sum game" worldviews, both of which are inclined to assume that the world is divided into black and white or friends and enemies. China's holistic worldview is inclined to assume otherwise and that everything in the world is interconnected.

Lao Tzu stated in the *Book of Dao* that "people should observe the world from a world perspective." In the ancient Chinese worldview, China was not China; it was the land under the heavens. The invasion of the West gave China a new identity; China became "China" and people were encouraged to consider the relationship that China had with the rest of the world.

In my opinion, the level of theoretical enlightenment achievable using Chinese philosophies to view the global system is unachievable using Western theories, and the sense of utopia is one that cannot be understood by narrow-minded interest-oriented scholars. If global systems were arranged based on the "zero-sum game" guidelines, universal chaos would be inevitable, and this is the reason for the current intense opposition to globalization. Adopting a liberal, global, collective approach to viewing the world is the main philosophy of global governance.

The concept of *tianxia* (天下; all under heaven) in traditional Chinese culture signifies geological space and value. During the late Ming and early Qing dynasties, Gu Yanwu provided a clear analysis of *guo* (国; dynasty) and *tianxia*. Gu stated that

> The collapse of *guo* is not synonymous with the collapse of *tianxia*. The collapse of *guo* refers to the changing of the dynasty, Emperor, or country's name. These problems are the concern of the Emperor and his ministers and stakeholders. The collapse of *tianxia* refers to the degradation of virtue and benevolence; although people may seem virtuous and benevolent on the surface, a regressed society of conflict is formed.

In other words, *guo* merely refers to the power of a dynasty, and *tianxia* is the order of civilizations. *Guo* can collapse, whereas *tianxia* must be maintained to prevent the world from falling into chaos.

The acquisition of *tianxia* theories is key to developing the *tianxia* value of "observing the world from a world perspective," which is an approach to or starting point for global governance. "Observing the world from a world perspective" refers to perceiving the world (*tianxia*) as a space of common resources for public politics and addressing world problems from a macro perspective. Only by perceiving the world as an indivisible a priori unit can the long-lasting benefits, values, and responsibilities of the world be identified and defined; this concept is the holism of global governance.

Holism emphasizes that human society is a community made up of all humans and the world is an aggregation of all countries and their peoples that belongs to everyone. Humans are commonly classified into various groups, ethnicities, races, ranks, interest groups, and types based on standards and indices. However, no single group, ethnicity, race, rank, interest group, or type can represent all of human society. People of different ranks from different countries and of different ethnicities have different interests. The purpose of global governance is to absolve these differences to prevent the world from falling into chaos.

After the disbandment of the Soviet Union and end of the Cold War, Samuel P. Huntington proposed the theory of civilizational clash and explained that civilizational conflict had replaced ideological conflict. Specifically, civilizational clash refers to the clash of Confucianism, Islam, and Christianity. Huntington concluded by stating that various civilizations deem themselves to be the center of the world and perceive other civilizations as hostile. Such perceptions may lead to ethnic hostilities and civilizational clash, thereby objectively destroying the basis of global value consensus.

Theorists of civilizational clash believe that civilizations are diverse, universal values are impossible to achieve, and conflict is inevitable. These theories raise the following questions: (1) Is holism unachievable? (2) Does it undermine civilizational diversity? (3) Is the harmonious global system based on holism a hypothesis?

First, holism is a product of Chinese civilization, and thus deviates from universal values. In holism, Chinese philosophies are centered on interrelationships between the heavens, the earth, and people. Concepts based on relationships rather than individuals form "views from everywhere" rather than "views from somewhere." This neutral approach to examining problems requires scholars to observe problems from the perspective of relationships rather than from that of individuals, and is therefore different from the individual-centered approach adopted in Western countries. Universal values are opposing and conflicting perspectives based on the logic of right and wrong and selection. Holism recognizes not only conflict but also that relationships are dynamic and that conflict can be absolved.

Second, China's philosophies encourage the establishment of world order rather than world dominance; the world must maintain a state of order, otherwise all things in it would offset one another, resulting in the loss of interest for everyone. China does not seek dominance and has always opposed "strongest takes all" values. From the perspective of relational ontology, the only method of maximizing the interest of one party in a two-way relationship is to maximize the interest of the other party.

Third, holism emphasizes the symbiosis of human societies. Coexistence is a norm not only in nature but also in human and global societies. Holism requires the participation, coordination, and cooperation of all entities involved in global trade governance. In other words, the world must collectively participate in the establishment of various systems such as the provision of public goods, formulation and implementation of public regulations, and control of public crises. Such measures highlight multiculturalism. The second value category based on holism is described in the following subsection.

Harmonious but different

Holism perspectives are not intended to disrespect individuals. The second tier of values strives to achieve harmony among societies and encourages societies to seek commonalities while remaining different. "Harmonious but different" values reflect the acceptance of one country, culture, or race to others.

To reiterate the aphorism proposed by Fei Xiaotong, "People must cherish their own values and appreciate the values of others. When all values come together, the world becomes a single unified entity." Fei examined the rationality of individual cultures and advocated the progression of cultural awareness to cultural assessment, and finally to the unification of universal values. His aphorism reflects a logical order that clearly expresses his thoughts and ideas.

First, Fei stated that "one should cherish his or her own values." Despite globalization, all ethnicities and countries and their civilizational development processes are historically unique. European and American scholars derived the "definition of civilization," and their perspective of viewing cultural differences as innate differences is biased and can lead to hatred. By contrast, Fei asserted that clear boundaries exist between countries, cultures, and regions amidst globalization. These boundaries are key for the structuring of societies because political, cultural, and regional entities rely on them to maintain internal order and form internal relationships (Fei, 2000).

Second, Fei started that "one should appreciate the values of others." This section of the aphorism refers to accepting other cultures in order to cooperate and coexist with them. People begin to understand, accept, and praise the values of others amidst frequent and equitable exchange.

Third, Fei stated that "all values should be consolidated." This section of the aphorism refers to a state where people not only tolerate the existence of different values and standards but also praise them. This state constitutes the progression from tolerance to acceptance, finally reaching a consensus toward cultural values; diversity gradually shifts toward uniformity. In this state, the meaning of "harmonious but different" becomes evident.

Finally, Fei stated that "the consolidation of values leads to unification." In this state, a set of universally accepted values is formed; many standards are consolidated into one, and the unification of *tianxia* is achieved.

The aphorism of Mr. Fei comprehensively highlights the course of evolution from individual cultures to *tianxia* unification. Fei believed that although all economies of the world are associated and codependent, humans remain culturally discriminant and lack a common set of values and standards. If this problem remains unresolved, humans are destined for chaos. To avoid chaos, humans must adhere to reason.

Mr. Fei's view on *tianxia* unification is consistent with the concept of holism in global governance proposed in this book. Consistency in this book refers to common objectives and values; it is a type of ideal. The difference between *tianxia* unification and holism is that holism is an ideal and a methodology. Specifically, it is an approach to realize personal ideals and a method to view world problems from a macro perspective. Only by steadily maintaining holism can *tianxia* unification ultimately be achieved.

The concept of "global governance" requires observers to view the future of the world from a holistic perspective and employ holistic approaches to resolve global issues with a view to forming a more valuable new world order. Global governance acknowledges the traditional, ethnicity- and country-centered view of order and encourages people to view human societies from a holistic perspective, involving governing and managing the survival and development of the global society as global public issues. Global governance urges analysts to analyze problems on a global scale. Therefore, a global system is essential for highlighting strong global responsibility and awareness. In a global institution, parties should adhere to multilateralism and abide by WTO objectives and principles, international laws, and recognized international relations guidelines in the existing economic trade system. All of these efforts are within the scope of holism. In other words, global governance can be achieved only through holism.

Win–win

International trade creates interest; this is a perpetual proposition of free trade theory. The subsequent allocation of interest created through international trade is a long-debated problem in international trade theories.

The most prominent manifestation of international trade is the aggressive unilateralism of the United States. Aggressive unilateralism adopts the power of international trade relationships to allocate international trade benefits. Bhagwati asserted that the United States uses Section 301 of the Trade Act to aggressively gain unilateral concessions from weaker trading partners. Aggressive unilateralism manifests as an abuse of power to extort trading benefits from weaker countries. Bhagwati also provided examples that validated the United States' use of Section 301 to gain trading concessions from Japan and South Korea (Bhagwati, 1996).

The extortion of trading benefits through the abuse of power remains evident in international trade, gradually stimulating a rise in protectionism. The allocation of interest in international trade is an increasingly core problem in global governance. In response, the multi-win and win–win values proposed by China are gradually gaining popularity in various countries.

We believe that equality is at the core of win–win values. Equilibrium is a product of interaction and mutual accommodation between various stakeholders. However, achieving equilibrium is extremely time-consuming. Similar to the periodicity of economic crises, the balancing of interests is a process that requires time to be uncovered.

The various relationships in global trade systems must be elucidated to benefit all entities equally. The current global governance system objectively comprises the "you or me," "winner takes all," "win more lose less," and "mutual demise" values because after World War II, the various entities within the system interacted with and influenced one another in a variety of manners. The United States exploited its dominance after World War II to establish an international system that served its purpose. In this system, developed countries were able to play to their economic strengths to establish "win more lose less" values. The "you or me," "winner takes all," and "win more lose less" values are manifestations of the imbalance among the interactive interrelationships between the various entities within the global system, and are also values that consider self-interest the sole reason to move forward.

In global trade governance, a balance of interest cannot be achieved by merely reaching a consensus at the global negotiations table or agreeing to a solution to a single problem. Potential benefits extend beyond the economic interests of countries, ethnicities, and interest groups sitting around a negotiation table. When companies involved in global governance reach a consensus, they may meet the interests of all or only a portion of the people. Therefore, countries must have a greater vision when discussing the balance of interests. The Obama administration believed that promoting TPP negotiations adhered to the interests of the United States. By contrast, the Trump administration believes that such negotiations do not benefit specific interests such as those of American workers and labor-intensive enterprises in the United States. During negotiations, many member countries were concerned regarding the interests of other stakeholders; for example, Australian farmers were concerned that open trade would affect their interests. Therefore, clarifying the interest relationships in global governance is a prerequisite for achieving a win–win situation. In a globalized international community, trading relationships manifest as interest. China's win–win ideology involves the creation of a system where interest relationships maintain harmony and conflict is minimized. Therefore, the concept of win–win represents achieving a balance between various interest relationships.

The present global system reflects a new trend of gradual integration and codependence among its member countries. In this balanced system framework, the pursuit of win–win values has become a trend.

Value contribution of China's trade governance

In this book, we propose three value elements, namely holism, harmonious but different, and win–win. These elements are intrinsically interconnected. Holism is the basis of the rationale herein, serving as a prerequisite for discussing the benefits of harmonious but different and win–win values.

The value contribution of China's trade governance stems from how it perceives global systems. Western and Eastern countries have different dreams of creating a global system. In individual-oriented Western cultures, values are absolute and universal. Therefore, from a Western perspective, assimilation is an effective means of forming peaceful global communities and global systems. In the holistic Chinese ideology, a global system is a whole that constantly interacts and changes during development. The evolution from relationships to codependence is the primary goal of becoming a global community. China deems events or systems as frameworks containing opposition and symbiosis. All entities within a system have various possible interrelationships. Under a holistic framework, parties should promote symbiosis in diverse and complex systems to form peaceful communities.

These cultural elements reflect the concept of the "three communities" characterized in China's B&R strategy, specifically the communities of shared interest, shared destiny, and shared responsibility. Western governance theories characterize the concept of the stakeholder and detail the interest structure of governance systems. Therefore, individual pursuits of self-interest are a hypothetical precondition of governance. The theory of the three communities encompasses the interest element. From a Chinese philosophical perspective, maximizing self-interest requires an individual to maximize the interests of others, which is a breakthrough from the value concepts of Western countries. The B&R strategy descriptions exceed simple interest, advocating the concept that "*tianxia* is *tianxia* for all," or the community of shared destiny.

5 Institutional arrangement of B&R trade governance

Definition of governance elements

Global governance essentially aims to provide a type of institutional arrangement. Global governance cannot be achieved without a set of universal rules that regulate all global citizens. An institutional arrangement comprises a series of system elements, each of which is separately discussed in this chapter. The elements are systems, rules, and processes. Institutional arrangement also contains value elements, which were discussed in the preceding chapter.

Rules

Under general circumstances, rules refer to habits, customs, ethics, laws, and policies. From a relational perspective, rules characterize commonalities and unity between habits, customs, ethics, laws, and policies. For example, although habits are dispersed and independent, they are formed unconsciously through interaction and life practices. In other words, habits are the rules of a free state and are generally perceived as crucial unspoken rules. Customs have more commonalities; they are the heritage of common knowledge and actions. Ethics involve greater awareness than do customs and constitute refined and revised common knowledge. Laws are rules for converting conscious knowledge to action that are implemented through enforcement. Compared with that of habits, customs, and ethics, the knowledge content of laws is more systematic and their action content is more procedural. Consequently, the effect of laws is obligatory. Policies are periodic goals, action principles, missions, methods, and procedures or measures standardized by countries or institutions through authority. In contrast to laws, policies have time constraints; they are explicit measures promoted within a specific time frame to meet specific historical or national conditions. Moreover, they are more flexible than laws.

The key rules of global trade governance are laws and policies. Trade agreements between various countries and the World Trade Organization (WTO) trade rules constitute the legal framework for global trade governance. The trade laws of various countries are also sources of global trade governance laws. To prepare for specific tasks in specific periods, countries form trade policies. These policies should conform to existing laws.

Systems

Although the concepts of global trade governance were introduced relatively recently in history, global trade systems have existed for thousands of years, spanning the Han dynasty, Roman Empire, and Silk Road eras. The development of global trade, particularly globalization, facilitated the formation of global trade systems and other institutional systems such as the tributary system in the East and colonial system in the West.

Global trade systems refer to the formation of economic and trade relations from systematic and regulated interactions between international bodies (mainly powerful countries). The formation of global trade systems was essential for the development of global trade. The US-led global trade system introduced after World War II featured many human-oriented constructs that led to the rise of numerous institutional arrangements such as multilateralism, regionalism, pluralism, bilateralism, and unilateralism.

After the inauguration of Donald Trump as president, the United States completely abandoned the multilateral trade system established after World War II, thereby once again destabilizing and restructuring the global trade system. The B&R was proposed during this period of instability. In contrast to President Trump allowing the global trade governance system to regress, President Xi Jinping of China publicly expressed China's support of the global multilateral system at the World Economic Forum held in Davos, Switzerland, in January 2017. Xi asserted that blindly blaming economic globalization for global issues is neither realistic nor helpful, and that we should take the initiative and enforce appropriate management to highlight the benefits of economic globalization, thereby rebalancing economic globalization processes.

Global trade systems involve multilateralism, regionalism, pluralism, bilateralism, and unilateralism, each of which can be selected for different system functions. In the change and restructuring processes of global trade systems, different countries may prefer different systems to gain the benefits produced by various system functions.

Multilateralism is a complex and content-rich system. A number of scholars have characterized systems with three or more participants as multilateral systems. In our opinion, multilateral systems imply the infinite expansion of participating entities, thereby constituting the closest system to a global system. Representative multilateral systems include the United Nations (UN) and WTO. At present, multilateralism is the closest system to a global system.

Renowned American political scientist Robert Keohane asserted that "Multilateralism refers to an institution comprising many countries. This institution helps countries realize their policies by providing specific institutional arrangements" (Keohane, 1994). Keohane believes that multilateralism is a product of specific institutional arrangements. He classifies multilateralism into three levels. The first level is instrumental multilateralism, which serves as a diplomatic or political tool. The second level is systemic multilateralism, which serves as a set of rules or a governing system. The third level is strategic multilateralism, which serves to promote diplomatic concepts and guide thinking. Chinese scholars have mostly agreed that multilateralism in global trade governance can serve as a basis for establishing global trade governance systems. They have also maintained that multilateralism is both a set of organizational principles and a set of governing concepts in the present global trade governance. Because of the number of participants in multilateralism, it is the closest system to a global system.

"Plurilateral" is a term used in the multilateral framework. Plurilateral agreements are trade agreements signed by three countries or more, thereby constituting pluralism. The lack of progress across broad areas of the current Doha Agenda negotiation has drawn attention to the possibility of smaller-scale negotiations, on a plurilateral basis, intended to promote a commonly shared agenda among like-minded countries. Plurilateral negotiations are normally expected to involve all major participants in a sector to the point of eliminating or substantially reducing the risk of "free riding," which normally implies that some 80% or 90% of the global market concerned is covered. Negotiations in the WTO are open in principle to all members, and consensus must be the main decision-making practice, as provided for in Article IX:1 of the WTO Agreement. Nevertheless, with the increasing diversity of issues and their complexity, reaching consensus has become more challenging. In many instances, negotiations have thus been conducted among a subset of the WTO membership, with the results being implemented on a most favored nation (MFN) basis. In other words, plurilateral negotiating processes have produced outcomes that potentially benefit all members. Such processes, by their very nature, do not need to be approved by the entire membership to start or conclude (Adlung and Mamdouh, 2016). I do think the plurilateral negotiation is the only realistic basis for moving the WTO trade system forward.

In contrast to pluralism, traditional regional trade agreements are based on specific regions. Regional trade agreements (RTAs) have risen in number and reach over the years, including a notable increase in large plurilateral agreements under negotiation. According to statistics released by the WTO, 455 regional trade agreements were in effect as of 2017. Non-discrimination among trading partners is one of the core principles of the WTO; however, RTAs constitute one of the exemptions and are authorized under the WTO, subject to a set of rules. What all RTAs in the WTO have in common is that they are reciprocal preferential trade agreements between two or more partners (Figure 5.1).

Bilateral trade governance is an earlier concept of trade governance that involves the trade relations and governance models of two countries. Bilateral governance is one of the earliest forms of global governance and a basis for the development of multilateral systems. The contributions of the United States to the development of postwar multilateral system legislation stemmed from its early bilateral agreement ideologies. Bilateral systems can coexist with multilateral and regional systems; in other words, various bilateral relations are present in multilateral and regional systems.

Unilateralism emerged as a personal gain system in global systems. Countries adopt unilateralism for self-preservation and for independently handling global trade affairs. Unilateralism is typically manifested in multilateral systems, where countries focus on personal gain, act independently, and ignore constraints established by international organizations, conventions, or alliances. Unilateralism is typically exhibited in dominant countries within an international community or those that have the capability to act independently.

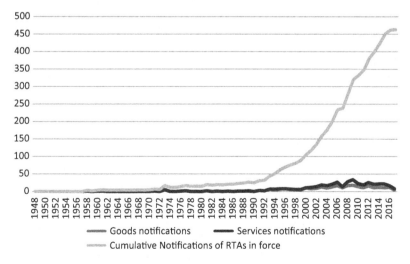

Figure 5.1 Evolution of regional trade agreements, 1948–2017
Source: World Trade Organization, 2017

Rules, systems, and order

Each disorganization of global trade systems results in an adjustment. During these adjustments, the scope, rules, and mechanisms of the trade system are expanded or merged to meet global governance trends.

Systems can be in one of two states: orderly or disorderly. When a system is orderly and has effective rules, it achieves a state of balance, thereby ensuring coordinated and stable growth. In global trade systems, order refers to consistencies and inconsistencies, and competition and cooperation between countries. When countries are in a state of cooperation, the system is orderly; otherwise, the system is in a state of disorder.

Processes

Global trade governance relies on collective actions to establish system rule processes.

Global governance essentially aims to provide a type of institutional arrangement, but cannot be achieved without a set of universal rules that regulate all global citizens. Therefore, a core issue of global governance is to establish systemic rules through the collective actions of various organizations and use these rules to influence and resolve global problems. Global trade governance is not a static system; it is a process that involves the collective actions of entities involved in global governance to establish and enforce rules and resolve disputes.

From a macro perspective of global trade governance, the entities involved include the primary sector (the government), secondary sector (multinational enterprises), and tertiary sector (nonprofit and nongovernment organizations). The operation of global trade governance relies on multilevel multidimensional cooperation networks and domestic and international processes. The governing process can be characterized into the stages of issue selection, advocacy, promotion, consensus formation, and agreement.

B&R and global trade systems

Fully understanding the difficulties of global system development

Because of uneven global political and economic development, imbalance and fluctuation are inevitable in global systems.

After two world wars, the order established by the British colonial system began to lose balance and rationality, and the various elements within the system began to shift toward the subsequent appropriately balanced system. Specifically, the GATT/WTO-based multilateral system created by the

United States achieved temporary balance. The trade governance system continued to evolve through the process of repeatedly losing and regaining balance. Global governance based on any existing system created problems related to identity asymmetry and interest imbalance for the countries involved in the system. Therefore, changes in the system were normal. We have now entered a period of system restructuring. China has proposed the B&R as a method of restructuring the global trade governance system. This proposal will inevitably create opportunities and difficulties.

Relationship between the B&R and existing multilateral systems

Contemporary international communities are not disorderly. On the contrary, they exhibit substantial international stability. Examples include the UN-centered international political order based on the Yalta system and free-trade or free-market-inspired WTO system. Essentially, these systems are controlled and maintained by the United States, and thus are sometimes referred to as "Pax Americana" systems. Since joining the WTO, China has been one of the greatest beneficiaries of the current international system. Therefore, China has not abandoned current multilateral system ideologies.

Aspects of the relationship between the B&R and multilateral system are detailed as follows. (1) The B&R respects the existing rules and frameworks of the multilateral system and has not been established to disrupt this system. On the contrary, China remains one of the strongest supporters of the existing multilateral system. (2) Based on the principles of the WTO, China should establish B&R trade governance theories that supplement, subdue, and innovate existing multilateral trade governance theories. (3) The advancement and progress of the B&R should perpetually abide by WTO rules and accept the constraints established by the WTO. B&R trade activities should be conducted on a global scale without geographical limitations. Therefore, B&R participants should accept the rules and constraints of the open cooperation system; for example, if two WTO member countries engage in bilateral cooperation, they should consciously abide by WTO rules and use the channels established by the WTO to resolve disputes. (4) The B&R constitutes a national trade strategy; it does not contain mandatory laws. Therefore, the existing rules of the WTO provide institutional support to the B&R.

Relationship between the B&R and regionalism

Scholars advocating regionalism have always emphasized that regionalism supplements multilateral systems and is the basis for new global rules in the 21st century. Section 24 of the GATT provides a legal basis for regional trade agreements. The WTO admitted the importance of regional agreements to the promotion of free trade. However, in certain situations, regionalism may not supplement multilateral trade systems but rather may negatively impact multilateral trade. Regional agreements do not offer the same open trade commitments to nonmember countries, and thus the MFN rules could be significantly and negatively affected. Regional agreements expand trade protectionism and facilitate geopolitics.

As a form of global trade governance, regionalism has political and economic significance. From the perspective of geopolitics, regionalism can be adopted as a tool to achieve strategic balance. After the Obama administration introduced the Trans-Pacific Partnership (TPP) and announced its intent to increase its cooperation with Asia-Pacific countries, China joined the Regional Comprehensive Economic Partnership (RCEP), B&R, and other regional arrangements to hedge the influence of regionalism exerted by the United States. This is an example of using regionalism as a tool for balance. From an economic perspective, regionalism can facilitate the balanced development of regional economies. Although global value chains have already been established, only independent industries exhibit globalized characteristics. Most industries such as agriculture and light industries exhibit regional cooperation characteristics. As part of regional value chains, these industries can achieve partial balance in global trade networks and correct imbalances in globalization.

Bilateralism as an experimental tool in the restructuring phase of global systems

Historically, bilateralism refers to free "constructs" in global trade, and is the starting point of multilateral systems. Therefore, bilateralism can shape systems. First, bilateral systems are fair and reciprocal, and system functions are simple and convenient. Thus, such systems effectively overcome the tediousness of multilateral negotiations. Second, bilateral systems contain specific legislative concepts that can be applied to the development of new systems; for example, reciprocity can be multilateralized to form the MFN principle for multilateral systems. Third, bilateral systems accommodate trial and error. During system restructuring, new trade and legislative concepts are proposed, and these concepts can be tested in bilateral systems. The cost of trial and error is considerably lower in bilateral systems than in other systems. Naturally, the bilateralism mentioned here does not refer to bilateral trade protection, but rather an initial system established during the restructuring of global systems or the bilateralism of free trade. The B&R is also based on a bilateral approach. China hopes to use bilateral systems as a means of testing global governance and learning through trial and error.

B&R rules

Challenges of global governance faced by developing countries

After World War II, a global economic and trade governance system led by the GATT, UN, and World Bank (all predecessors of the WTO) was formed. However, the problems encountered during the development of this system were not properly addressed. Abuse of power emerged during the first round of GATT negotiations, where trade negotiations centered on the interests of developed countries. The greatest beneficiaries of developing countries, namely the textile and agriculture industries, were expelled from the negotiation table. In the 1980s, developing countries actively participated in the Uruguay Round; however, the effects of the agreements made during the Uruguay Round failed to meet the expected outcomes characterized during trade negotiations. Consequently, many countries became poorer, leading to a regression in global trade. The Doha Development Round was held in 2001 at the growing demand of developing countries to resolve the unfairness inherent in global economic and trade governance. These negotiations were seemingly focused on resolving development problems. However, progress remains stagnant to this day; developed countries have yet to show their commitment to resolving development issues.

The scope of governance of the UN Conference on Trade and Development (UNCTAD) is wider than that of the WTO. However, the UNCTAD has neither a stringent negotiation schedule nor the power to form international legislation. The goal of the UNCTAD is to promote trade and economic development among UN member countries, particularly developing countries. The conference also focuses on maximizing trade, investment, and development opportunities in developing countries, thereby helping these countries to cope with the challenges of globalization and fairly integrate their economies into the world economy; formulating principles and policies to resolve international trade and economic development problems; and proposing action plans. The UNCTAD's primary scope of operation encompasses (1) products and trade, (2) investment and corporate development, (3) macroeconomic policy formulation and debt/development financing, and (4) technology and logistics. The UNCTAD endeavors to utilize the resources of developing countries to facilitate their participation in global economic and trade governance. Terms of preferential treatment for developing countries were previously formulated at the conference, thereby helping developing countries secure universal concessions.

The World Bank provides funds and technical support to developing member countries to improve their productivity and promote economic development and social progress. The governance tools employed by the World Bank include (1) providing existing or raised capital and resources as funds for production, thereby providing supplementary support for the lack of private investments; (2) using endorsements, providing private loans, or participating in other private investments to promote private foreign investments; and (3) encouraging international investments to help member countries enhance productivity, quality of life, and labor conditions. The World Bank adopts international finance and investments as a governance tool to promote economic development in developing countries. However, the provision of loans to developing countries interferes with domestic economics. Therefore, this approach has been met by opposition from developing countries.

In addition to the global economic and trade governance products provided by the aforementioned three major international economic and trade organizations, other multilateral cooperation mechanisms also provide developing countries with necessary global governance products; examples of such mechanisms include the Shanghai Cooperation Organisation, Asia-Pacific Economic Cooperation, China-ASEAN (10+1) Free Trade Area, Greater Mekong Subregion Economic Cooperation Program, Asia-Europe Meeting, China–Arab States Cooperation Forum, and Asia Cooperation Dialogue. However, these products are not notably effective because of the sheer number of mechanisms and the diversity of their goals. In US-led global governance, developed countries decide the intentions and value of global governance, resulting in a severe parting of global governance objectives between countries in the Northern and Southern Hemispheres. Developed countries control the formulation of global governance rules, causing these rules to lack rationality and coordination. President Xi stated that "Developed countries have always led global political and economic order. This has created issues of hegemonism, unilateralism, and north-south segregation." Therefore, correcting the long-standing deviation, ineffective approaches, and failed outcomes in global economic and trade governance is imperative.

With the decline in power of the United States, global governance has become centered on enhancing self-interest, reducing public goods expenditure, and decreasing or suspending the global provision of public goods. Scholars have estimated that the infrastructure support funds raised by the multilateral development banks and the governments of developed countries will be able to satisfy only 2% to 3% of the fund requirements of developing countries. President Xi noticed the changes in the statuses of the countries involved in global governance and asserted that the reform of global governance systems is at a historical transitioning point. The balance of international power is changing significantly. Emerging markets and countries and many developing countries are rapidly growing and expanding their international influence. This situation marks the greatest change in the balance of international power in recent times.

Setting common development goals

The globalization characterized in the B&R constitutes the process of rebalancing globalization. The historical mission was to achieve balanced development in globalization and incorporate peripheral countries into the global system through globalization. This round of globalization should involve the promotion of mutual development, which is also the economic objective of China's B&R economic and trade governance.

Amidst the gradual regression of US-led globalization, we have identified an opportunity to restructure the system into one that promotes development. This opportunity could become the driving force that promotes the economic development of B&R coastal countries. B&R trade governance focuses on mutual development and urges countries to abandon US-led global governance ideologies. This is one aspect of the governance theories established by China based on the B&R.

First, mutual development subdues the concepts of literalism governance. Mutual development concepts do not deny the progressive significance of literalism but rather accept the positive effects of freedom of trade and investment while heeding the negative factors of literalism. Mutual development concepts recognize that developing countries are oppressed in globalization and their statuses have been exploited within the order of globalization. Mutual development concepts exceed simple free trade objectives, prioritizing economic development in global governance to accommodate more countries.

Second, in a traditional sense, mutual development concepts do not imply resolutions for survival issues but rather aim to resolve development issues. "Development," as characterized in the WTO negotiations framework, often refers to agricultural problems or the survival of poor countries. In this book, we refer to development as mutual development with the objective of industrialization: a higher level of development. A key pathway for developing countries to achieve economic growth is to achieve industrialization. The American economist Simon Kuznets examined industrialization from the perspective of the conversion angle of resource allocation structures and defined industrialization as the primary domain of resource allocation, where agriculture industries transition into other industries. Kuznets asserted that industrialization refers to the "origins of products and destinations of resources that shifted agricultural activities to non-agricultural activities." Variety in national trade strategies and policies is the main reason for varying levels of industrialization. The B&R aims to create opportunities for developing countries to grow through strategy and policy formulation.

Third, setting appropriate mutual development governance objectives helps B&R countries identify their economic development priorities and choose suitable development models, policies, and tools. Many developing countries withdraw into the safety of nationalism and protectionism during periods of globalization regression or the stagnation of global economic and trade governance. China aims to actively explore the common interests of developing countries and identify opportunities for development through the B&R. China believes that it has sufficient factor endowments, industrial advantages, and investment ability to promote the industrial development and industrialization of B&R coastal regions, and also that such efforts meet the needs of regular market investments. Developing countries are in the initial stages of industrialization. Therefore, they require investment in light industry and infrastructure, which gives China an advantage.

Fourth, from the long-term perspective, the implementation of B&R economic and trade governance with the objective of mutual development will generate new global governance ideologies and institutional arrangements. Global economic and trade governance has failed to resolve development issues. The innovations proposed in the B&R have gained substantial approval by the UN. The UN acknowledges that the objectives, philosophies, and pathways advocated in the B&R are consistent with its plans for continued development. The promotion and early fulfillment of the B&R would be a key contribution to the continued development objectives of the UN. The focus of the B&R is to promote trade investment between China and coastal countries and interconnect these countries to achieve a new age of industrialization, thereby benefiting coastal residents. These objectives coincide with the continued development objectives of the UN. We believe that in periods of stagnated global economic and trade governance, the B&R could become a source of public goods in global governance.

B&R trade governance principles: a recommendation

Principles are the core legal elements in a rule system and also the foundation of rule systems. The United Kingdom and United States apply different base principles when forming different rule systems.

The trade systems adopted by the United Kingdom can be characterized into two stages: the unilateral free trade system in the 19th century and the imperial preferential system in the 20th century. In the 19th century, the United Kingdom's emerging bourgeoisie advocated unilateral free trade.

Other countries had yet to acknowledge the benefits of free trade or form free trade ideologies. The free trade system developed in the United Kingdom accommodated unilateral and bilateral free trade. Under a unilateral system, the United Kingdom maintained free trade with countries regardless of whether these countries were willing to trade freely with them. Under a bilateral system, free trade was "reciprocal." The United Kingdom asserted that reciprocity should not be overly emphasized in policies, claiming that reciprocal terms and conditions would be manipulated by overseas trade protectionists and exploited for personal gain, and reciprocal tariffs would subsequently render dissuading other countries from being open to free trade more difficult.

The United Kingdom's economic and technological superiority gradually waned in the 20th century, particularly after the capitalist economic crisis of 1932, which forced the United Kingdom to replace its long-standing free trade policies with trade protection policies. Meanwhile, the United Kingdom formed an imperial preferential system of tariff alliances with its colonies and self-governing territories. Similar to the unilateral free trade system of the United Kingdom, the United States emphasized "reciprocity" in its trade policies.

The principle of reciprocity is considered as a pillar of the multilateral trading system. Bagwell and Staiger explain that "the principle of reciprocity in the GATT/WTO refers to the ideal of mutual changes in trade policy that bring about changes in the volume of each country's imports that are of equal value to changes in the volume of its exports" (Bagwell and Staiger, 2002). Thus, concessions are balanced or reciprocated when they result in equivalent changes in bilateral trade flows. Although it is nowhere defined explicitly, reciprocity in the GATT/WTO has always been understood in this way.

Reciprocity is neither simply free trade nor protection but rather symbolizes a "carrot and stick" system. Reciprocal free trade refers to free trade based on other's actions. Specifically, reciprocal free trade policies are based on mutual concessions, and the parties involved in such policies must agree to lower their trade barriers. Reciprocal free trade is a type of conditional free trade that sometimes trends toward protectionism.

A commendable part of the history of the United States trade governance is the establishment of the nondiscrimination principle. After World War II, the United States designed a postwar global economic and trade system. During this period, the imperial preferential system was the United Kingdom's core right of discourse. As the new global power, the United States abolished the preferential system and institutional goals based on discrimination. At the Atlantic Conference and Charter in 1941, the United States pushed to introduce the nondiscrimination principle. However, the proposal was refused by then UK Prime Minister Winston Churchill. Although the United States' aspiration to define "nondiscrimination" in the 1941 Atlantic Charter did not come to fruition, the charter characterized fair treatment in global trade, thereby cementing the development orientation of the postwar international trade system and establishing a basis for subsequent multilateral negotiations. This was the first victory for the United States in designing the postwar multilateral system. After World War II, the nondiscrimination principle became the core ideology of the global economic and trade governance of the United States.

The principle of special and differential treatment (SDT) is a special provision imposed by the WTO that granted developing countries special privileges and required developed countries to form preferential policies to help developing countries. Those opposed to this provision insist that such policies violate the principles of reciprocal negotiations, and thus could lead to protectionism. Others contend that if developing countries gain immunity, they may opt to gradually withdraw from global systems and close their doors to free trade. In our opinion, from the perspective of economic inequality in the contemporary world, fair laws should be incorporated into a global governance system that aims to achieve sovereign equality for all countries, thereby facilitating the formation of effective SDT principles. This is not only a requirement of the principle of sovereign equality of states in global governance but also an inevitable trend in the gradual development of international law.

SDT is deemed an exception in the GATT/WTO framework. At most, SDT is a principle that must be followed to resolve problems stemming from developing countries. The reason may be that as a tool for free trade, the GATT/WTO framework is comparable to traditional international laws in that these organizations essentially operate to maintain the interests of developed Western countries.

We recommend that B&R governance principles draw on the legislative content of the SDT principle to overcome past ex gratia and reciprocity limitations and provide B&R coastal developing countries with SDT. We also recommend defining the basic principles of B&R trade governance to operate under the MFN and SDT principles simultaneously. This approach highlights China's high valuation of the south-south cooperation model.

Stiglitz asserted that

> At present, a third of all global trade is done by developing countries. Trade between developing countries, or trade based on south – south cooperation, has grown twice as much as global trade. However, many restrictions still hinder south – south cooperation. For example, the tariffs for manufacturing imports between Latin American countries are

roughly seven times that of developed countries. Similarly, the tariffs for trade between Southeast Asian countries are roughly 60% higher than those of developed countries. In fact, if developing countries were to allow mutual market access, even greater profit could be created.

(Stiglitz, 2008)

Stiglitz believes that south-south cooperation is not progressing sufficiently quickly and countries should formulate solutions that center on south-south cooperation negotiations (Stiglitz, 2008). The emphasis of SDT in B&R governance is on establishing a set of rules to facilitate south-south cooperation.

Understanding the B&R policy principles of cobusiness, coconstruction, and sharing

At the opening ceremony of the 2015 Boao Forum for Asia held in Boao, Hainan, President Xi stated that B&R emphasizes the policy principles of cobusiness, coconstruction, and sharing. These principles are the pragmatic principles of B&R strategies and play a key role in global governance. A report released at the 19th National Congress of the Communist Party of China validated that the Chinese government's "global governance values are based *on* cobusiness, coconstruction, and sharing," insisting that all countries are equal, regardless of size, power, and wealth. The Chinese government supports the UN in actively expanding the representativeness and influence of developing countries in international affairs.

The Secretary of Foreign Affairs of the People's Republic of China, Zhang Yesui, discussed the aforementioned three principles in his 2015 written compilation. Zhang mentioned that "cobusiness" refers to brainstorming, considering the interests of various parties, and fully expressing their wisdom and creativity. All matters from the conceptualization and proposal stages to the advancement and reward stages are collectively discussed by coastal countries. "Coconstruction" refers to fulfilling coparticipation and maximizing advantages and potential to form new cooperative advantages. Coastal countries have various strengths that can be harnessed and collectively utilized. "Sharing" refers to creating win–win situations by identifying beneficial opportunities and the greatest common denominator for cooperation. This process is similar to collectively baking a large cake and then fairly and reasonably sharing the cake among the bakers (Zhang, 2015). The preceding discussion shows that the principles of cobusiness, coconstruction, and sharing are not strictly geared toward supporting laws but rather are overall action principles for the B&R or a set of cooperation principles.

Current global trade governance is led by dominant countries that advocate aggressive progression and concerted action, adopting models of treaty formulation and sovereignty transference. Such models are effective for forming strong law frameworks, and thus serve as processes for establishing restrictive rules. During the establishment of the WTO, the United States incorporated some trade concepts into the multilateral rule system. These concepts are primarily reflected in the basic principles of the WTO's rule system. The three principles proposed by China are those for promoting the B&R rather than establishing mandatory rules. They are the soft rules for nonformal cooperation models. These principles and the basic principles of the WTO's rule system are different in certain aspects and similar in others.

Constraints of B&R governance rules

Up to this point, we have discussed the values, objectives, and principles concerning the establishment of B&R rules. In addition to these aspects, our discussion also addresses relevant rules, or specific laws and policies. The B&R is not centered on international negotiations but rather focuses on bilateral or regional development while forming various agreements and policies that gradually shape its rules. In this book, we focus not on these specific rules but on the constraints imposed by the B&R.

The initial discussion focuses on existing international agreements. Existing global trade agreements include goods trading rules, service trading rules, and intellectual property. In global value chain theory, certain regional trade agreements encompass even more content. From border measures to beyond-border measures, such agreements have not only focused on the free trading of goods and services but have also encompassed new content such as trade facilitation, investment rules, economic and technological cooperation, competition rules, State owned enterprises, environmental policies, and labor provisions. A number of free trade agreement (FTAs) have focused on not only trade rules but also the integration of trade, investment, and service rules and the design of policies based on value chain theories. Existing rules and their development trends are adopted as a basis for establishing B&R rules.

The second discussion focuses on the development of developing countries. During the process of economic globalization, developing countries routinely fail to meet their economic development goals. Generally, economic development strategies adopted by developing countries emphasize enhancing industrialization. Therefore, the B&R should primarily focus on how to apply governance tools to facilitate economic development.

The governance-related problems encountered by developing countries are detailed as follows: (1) Diminishing economic sovereignty due to countries that sign international agreements being required to sacrifice a portion of their sovereignty. In other words, the interests of developing countries are not fully protected in international agreements. (2) Multinational corporations eroding the economies of developing countries through national investment activities. To some extent, multinational corporations control key economic departments in their host countries, monopolize products and markets, and affect the formulation of national economic policies, thereby influencing the development performance of their host countries. (3) The trade protection of developing countries is at risk. Some developed countries abuse their dominant status in international trade through measures such as requesting "voluntary trade restrictions" or other "gray" measures to force trade negotiations in their favor, thereby reducing the impact of competitive products on the exports of developed countries. The aforementioned problems are only a few of those encountered by developing countries. The establishment of B&R rules should focus on resolving these problems.

The third discussion focuses on the interest of China. B&R rules should satisfy the demands of domestic economic development in China. The balance between cost and interest must be considered during the establishment process. By taking advantage of the opportunities created by the B&R, China must actively establish productive international partnerships with coastal countries and form regional value chains. Such chains could not only satisfy the economic development requirements of coastal countries but also expand China's production capacity and optimize domestic industrial structures, thereby converting market-to-capital and technology exchanges to capital and technology-to-industry development exchanges. This is the economic development demand of the B&R, the rules of which should reflect this demand.

System establishment requires funding. Offsetting system costs and system income is extremely difficult because building a system is an extremely slow process that renders determining the cost of building a system extremely difficult. The financial contribution of a country to international organizations is easy to calculate; however, calculating the cost of garnering full public support is impossible. Therefore, the cost of establishing a system must be considered. Some system costs are intangible and can be absorbed by the market; for example, public support can be garnered through corporate-private exchanges. Such subtleties could facilitate the promotion of the B&R.

Establishment of B&R rules

Advocacy

A core problem of global trade governance is determining how to collectively establish system rules to resolve global issues. Actions include defining global issues, advocating policy recommendations, promoting policy recommendations, engaging in international negotiations, and achieving consensus. These actions are executed in two stages, namely domestic execution and international execution.

Global trade governance is diverse. The Commission on Global Governance (2005) believes the product of the handling of common public and personal affairs by various individuals and groups. Governance is a constant process where the reconciliation of conflict and difference between interested parties can be expected and cooperation can be achieved. Governance is a diversified concept that acknowledges hegemonism but aspires to develop multipolarization, multiagenting, and diversified governance. These development processes involve empowering recognized organizations or authorities to enforce necessary actions to achieve public or group consensus or form agreements based on the interests of all parties.

From a global trade governance perspective, China's B&R strategy is in an initial, diverse, multiprocess stage called the advocacy stage. Using policy advocacy as a participation model for establishing policy agendas constitutes the initialization of global governance. B&R trade governance also starts with advocacy.

Domestic advocacy

The domestic advocacy process of the B&R between 2012 and October 2013 can be characterized into four stages. The first stage was policy debate. Before the 18th National Congress of the Communist Party of China, policy makers and scholars fiercely debated the gains and losses of previous diplomatic efforts with neighboring countries and explored solutions to improve China's diplomatic policies. These were bottom-up discussions voluntarily convened by Chinese politicians and scholars, and they constituted the first step in advocacy. The second stage was policy establishment and adjustment. The "Neighbors First" diplomatic strategy and concept of a "community of shared destiny" were proposed at the 18th National Congress of the Communist Party of China. The third stage was advocacy separation. Within a year after the 18th National Congress, President Xi and Premier Li Keqiang proposed several neighboring and regional economic cooperation projects during overseas visitations. The fourth stage was initial closure. In October 2013, President Xi discussed "One Belt" and "One Road" as a single unified concept for the first time at the first Central Government Peripheral Diplomacy Forum. This marked the initial completion of domestic advocacy.

International advocacy

Once the initial closure of B&R policies had been achieved, these policies became China's key foreign policies during its initial stages of international advocacy. The policies are detailed as follows. (1) President Xi introduced the B&R during diplomatic events and international forums and to country leaders. (2) Scholars were major international promotors of the B&R, with increased publication of B&R-related research and presentation of B&R ideologies in international academic conferences and discussions. (3) Foreign affairs representatives of international organizations such as the UN approved of China's B&R content. In March 2016, the UN passed Resolution 2274, which specified the promotion of B&R content. The B&R was written into Resolution A/71/9 in the UN General Assembly for the first time, garnering the approval of 193 countries, thereby demonstrating the universal support of the international community for promoting the B&R. (4) Enterprises have consciously applied B&R concepts during corporate negotiations. In addition, several enterprises have created business opportunities centered on the B&R. Such efforts of corporate entities have enhanced the market understanding of B&R coastal countries. (5) Private organizations and individuals have promoted B&R concepts through travel and cultural exchanges. (6) Reports published by Chinese media in various countries have reinforced the advocacy of B&R policies.

Innovation of China's B&R advocacy

China's strategy is to present the B&R to the many countries involved in the trade system through advocacy. This strategy is unprecedented in the history of global trade governance for the following reasons. (1) In global trade governance, B&R advocacy touches on the core concepts of policies. Therefore, it is a type of concept advocacy. Global trade policies include normative policies as well as the philosophies and values of these policies. Consequently, values are the fundamental elements of policies. Currently, globalization is experiencing a developmental shift; people's free trade consensus has wavered. The B&R proposed to continue promoting economic cooperation and upholding free trade concepts, thereby strengthening the core concepts of and fundamentally supporting global trade governance. Moreover, the B&R respects multipolarized development, acknowledges the coexistence of various civilizations, and endeavors to achieve win–win outcomes. The B&R provides solutions for nationalism and zero-sum game problems in a period of anti-globalization, thereby significantly contributing to global trade systems. (2) The advocacy of the B&R reflects openness and tolerance; the B&R not only relies on existing global trade governance mechanisms but also expands them. Therefore, such advocacy is practical and innovative. The advocacy of the B&R does not aim to replace the failed global trade governance mechanisms of the WTO but rather recover existing cooperation mechanisms and realize new ones (e.g., EAEU-China FTAs, ASEAN-China FTAs) in the future. (3) The advocacy of the B&R

establishes a coalition of advocacy functions within systems. Advocacy creates publicity and promotes ideology recognition and alliance integration in policy formulation processes. The initial stage of B&R advocacy is the introduction of B&R by country leaders in international meetings. Subsequently, various mechanisms are applied to expand B&R concepts and the outcomes are reported in various media outlets. This advocacy process will trigger discussion of framework-related topics and resonate with international communities, leading to the application of common interest and realization of broad consensus.

Connectivity

A common policy concept often raised in B&R discussions is "connectivity," which is an innovative public commodity in China's global trade governance system.

Connectivity is a policy term used to describe the following concepts. (1) The connectivity of national or regional development strategies: in China, government-run media outlets often publish reports on B&R and the integration of national and regional development strategies in other countries, such as that of Kazakhstan's "Nurzhol Boulevard," Mongolia's "Steppe Road," and China's B&R. Many countries have proposed development plans similar to the B&R and such plans could potentially be merged with the B&R, examples including Indonesia's "Global Maritime Axis" national development plan, South Korea's "Eurasia Initiative," and Vietnam's "Two Corridors and One Economic Circle" plan, all of which are intended to connect with China's B&R. Countries are the main entities involved in the merging of China's B&R and national and regional development strategies of other countries. Such efforts are generally exerted by governments, and their economic content extends beyond trade and involves national economic development models. Such mergers based on connectivity are typically disclosed in diplomatic cooperation declarations and memorandums. They validate the supportive attitudes and willingness to cooperate of both parties. However, connectivity has relatively weak legal binding power. (2) FTA connectivity: B&R-EAEU connectivity is a classic example of FTA connectivity, another being the escalated negotiations of FTAs, which was mentioned in the China-Singapore Memorandum of Understanding. FTA connectivity is promoted by governments and involves China's national and regional involvement with countries that have existing FTAs or those that have signed FTAs with China. Most of these connections are focused on upgrading the content of existing international agreements, and their improvement promotes the formation of new international agreements. Therefore, such connections have strong legal binding power. (3) The connectivity of international organizations: UN

Resolution 2344 presented the key concept of a "community of shared destiny" for the first time, thereby validating the consensus of the international community and highlighting the significant contribution that China's concepts and solutions have had on global governance. The term "connectivity" applied by the UN refers to the successful integration of China's B&R and the UN's resolution by addressing issues concerning Afghanistan. Connecting with international organizations is a form of multilateral connectivity or a manifestation of the multilateralism of B&R strategies. Gaining the approval of the UN constitutes a major advancement in legitimizing the B&R internationally through multilateralization. Such connections include those between countries and those between international organizations. (4) Commercial project connectivity: the introduction of China's B&R facilitated the formation of the "five connections" cooperation model. Chinese enterprises have consolidated the "Go Out" policy and B&R and have connected the enterprises and business projects of B&R coastal countries. These connections primarily involve enterprises. The behaviors of these connections are market behaviors, where enterprises use B&R connections in their own interest. (5) The connectivity of local and departmental policies: since the introduction of the B&R by the Chinese government, each province has confirmed its status and external cooperation model in the B&R. For example, Xinjiang is distinguished as the core region in the Silk Road Economic Belt, focusing on national exchange and cooperation with countries and regions in Central, Southern, and Western Asia. Fujian is distinguished as the core region in the 21st Century Maritime Silk Route Economic Belt, focusing on cooperation with Southeast Asia and Taiwan. Furthermore, local governments have successively proposed solutions for B&R connectivity. In addition, various ministries and commissions have structured connectivity plans around work items. Although these connections primarily involve the Central Government, local governments and government-run departments have no diplomatic power; their connectivity policies and documents must be consistent with those of the Central Government.

Connectivity is not a traditional term used in relation to global economic and trade governance. Almost no countries have used this term when addressing international economic and trade affairs; China is the first country to propose the use of connectivity in this context. Therefore, connectivity is a public commodity provided by the B&R for global trade governance. The Chinese government has not provided a definition for connectivity. We attempted to conceptualize the policy implications of the term; based on current affairs, we identified the following characteristics of B&R connectivity.

First, a prerequisite of connectivity is that the other country involved must have a development strategy or corresponding cooperation mechanism. Only when both countries meet this prerequisite can they engage in subsequent cooperation. This deviates from the trade negotiations of the WTO, most of which concern new topics; one country raises a topic and other countries respond, thereby initiating a new round of negotiations. This is a creative negotiation model employed to establish new rules. Connectivity entails diplomatic coordination based on mutual respect for existing policy frameworks to identify opportunities for cooperation. Connectivity not only facilitate the process of establishing rules, it could also simply serve as a form of connected cooperation; for example, connecting FTZs could stimulate the establishment of new rules.

Second, connectivity is based on interest. The Chinese government often emphasizes that connections are established at a point in time that benefits China's B&R and the development strategies of other countries. These points of opportunity refer to a point in time that benefits development strategies by creating interests for the parties involved. Such interest has two levels of meaning in terms of connectivity: one is respect for other parties' interests and the other is the cocreation of new interest through connectivity.

Third, parties involved in connectivity comprise advocates and responders or policy implementers and receivers. These classifications clarify the dominant function of advocates in the connection process. Although connectivity is a mutual process, main processes and subprocesses exist. China undoubtedly serves as an advocate or implementer. Therefore, China must be capable of leading connectivity and implementing strategies for future connections, and should tactically employ proactive or aggressive policies.

Fourth, the content of connectivity is expansive and complex. According to current implementation progress, China employs connectivity strategies in its business projects, national development plans, FTZ establishment, and road, bridge, and rail construction. Its heavy reliance on connectivity renders the content of connectivity extremely vast and complex. This constitutes an initial manifestation of B&R economic and trade governance theories. If China aspires to transform connectivity into a public commodity that can be applied in global governance systems, it must first clearly characterize the content of connectivity and create categories for the conceptualized content. Nonetheless, ambiguity is normal during the initial stages of governance.

Fifth, connectivity is a form of diplomatic coordination and economic collaboration. Connectivity refers to the coordination of national economic affairs through diplomacy and is a form of governance that pursues mutual development. Diplomatic coordination is peaceful and voluntary, whereas economic collaboration is the practice of connectivity. These aspects highlight the economic attributes of B&R strategies. Notably, the B&R covers a greater scope of content than does the WTO, which focuses on trade, whereas the B&R focuses on economic development.

Few studies on global trade governance have provided a clear definition of connectivity or applied connectivity to examine B&R performance. Therefore, we produced the following definition of "connectivity" as a public commodity for global governance.

Connectivity is a policy term for global trade governance used by China to promote the B&R. Connectivity emphasizes respect for the existing economic development strategies of various regions and nations and the application of corresponding cooperation mechanisms to encourage interest sharing and economic coordination between connected countries, thereby achieving mutual development.

Multilateralism

Multilateralism is the approach adopted to legitimize the B&R internationally. This approach comprises the following three aspects.

1   Establishing a multilateral system that offers B&R services: China successfully launched the Asian Infrastructure Investment Bank (AIIB). The AIIB highlights China's support of and contribution to global governance in a period of stagnant global multilateralism. The success of the AIIB is attributed to China's multilateral ideologies. China has always promoted a regulated global governance system, the success of which has provided a financial support framework for the B&R. This approach should be sustained because it ensures international legitimacy. The launch of this system provided institutional legitimacy on an international scale. Therefore, the system is essentially a "self-improvement" system that advocates the evolution of international systems.

2   Achieving multilateralism through connectivity: American scholar John Ruggie proposed the concept of embedded multilateralism. Ruggie stated that the postwar multilateral system designed by the United States satisfied various domestic interventions in the United States. The experience of the Great Depression has made countries recognize national interventions as governance models for stabilizing their domestic economies. Therefore, multilateral designs must coincide with domestic economic development and safety objectives, and thus a "protection mechanism" is often incorporated into the design of multilateral trade systems. Such mechanisms take the form of exceptions in the process of promoting free trade and tariff reduction, and ensure that the interests of different countries are protected. Ruggie strongly believed that the core objective of postwar currency and trade mechanisms was

to develop a liberal system that coincided with and was restricted by domestic interventions, claiming that such a system could concurrently ensure the stability of international and domestic economies. The current multilateral system withstood the 2008 financial crisis and the revival of nationalism amidst Great Depression–like panic. Therefore, referencing the theory of embedded multilateralism is beneficial for promoting the B&R. The essence of embedded multilateralism is to regulate international mechanisms and the domestic interests of different countries. Embedded multilateralism serves to embed domestic interests into international mechanisms or international conventions. In actuality, China has gained considerable experience in promoting the B&R, and has proposed solutions to connect existing mechanisms with existing protocols. Collectively, these solutions form an embedding system to meet the demands of domestic interests.

3   Using existing international mechanisms to promote the B&R: China has gained the recognition of the UN. On 17 March 2017, Resolution 2344 to resolve the Afghanistan problem was passed at the UN General Meeting by 15 votes. The resolution called on the international community to help Afghanistan, and focuses on the B&R and other initiatives to reinforce regional economic cooperation, urge countries to provide safe environments for B&R construction, reinforce the connectivity of development policies and strategies, and promote interoperability and pragmatic cooperation.

In this book, we propose an embedded multilateral structure. The core aspect of embedded multilateralism is to regulate international mechanisms and the domestic interests of different countries by embedding these interests into international mechanisms or international conventions. We believe that China has ample experience in promoting the B&R. The features of the Chinese embedded B&R strategy based on bilateral pathways are illustrated in Figure 5.2.

The pathways established by the B&R system are different from those established by the RCEP and TPP.

Cedric Dupont asserted that the RCEP adopts a "matryoshka" embedding arrangement, where each layer can be independent or one part of a group, and has its own set of internal rules. Although the overall system grows as more countries become involved, the uniqueness of each layer renders the entire system diverse. The TPP is a series of multidynamic combinations, where each layer gradually expands as more members become involved. Moreover, the layers may expand to encompass new topics. The internal rules of each layer gradually decrease and are replaced by a universal set of rules to regulate all members. This arrangement focuses on eliminating

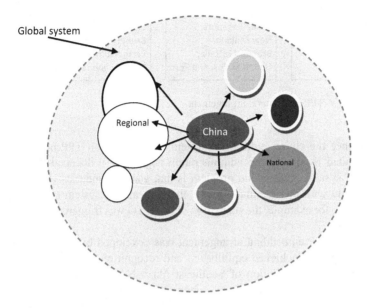

Figure 5.2 B&R embedded multilateralism

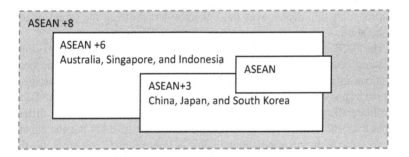

Figure 5.3 RCEP embedded arrangement

diversity. The multilateral arrangements of the RCEP and TPP are illustrated in Figures 5.3 and 5.4, respectively.

A dynamic multilateral arrangement is a classic American multilateral approach based on a dominant country and dominant rule system. This arrangement is expandable, as are the rule schedules and members. However, this approach has two major problems; the first is that dominant countries are in control of change; a change in policy preference may negatively

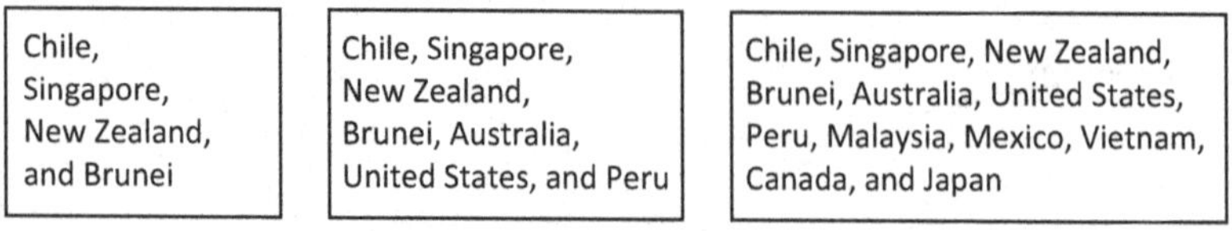

Chile, Singapore, New Zealand, and Brunei	Chile, Singapore, New Zealand, Brunei, Australia, United States, and Peru	Chile, Singapore, New Zealand, Brunei, Australia, United States, Peru, Malaysia, Mexico, Vietnam, Canada, and Japan

Figure 5.4 TPP multilateral arrangement

influence the entire multilateral system. The change in TPP negotiations scheduled by the Trump administration negatively influenced the multilateral system. The second problem is that game boundaries change concurrently with the dominant power, thereby causing system expansion to stagnate; for example, the stagnation of the WTO was triggered by dynamic variables.

The RCEP embedding arrangement was developed by small countries. This approach achieved equilibrium and recognition of rules in the core circle of the Association of Southeast Asian Nations (ASEAN), gaining acceptance in the international community. Multilateral systems originating in smaller countries are more tolerant and diverse, and the unification and expansion of rules become less crucial. If the ASEAN serves as the intermediate facilitator in the continuous multilateral system, its ability to control rules diminishes over time, thereby jeopardizing the future of the association.

The B&R differs from the RCEP and TPP. Currently, the B&R exhibits bilateral cooperation between China and several other countries and connections established between China and various FTAs. From the perspective of a sponsor country, China does not have the capacity to promote B&R multilateralism through hegemony, and in this manner the B&R differs from the TPP. When viewed as a single entity, the ASEAN has the capacity to serve as an intermediate facilitator or hub. When China promotes the B&R as an initiative rather than a binding negotiation schedule, the country serves as the core advocate of the B&R. From the perspective of rule dispersion capacity, the RCEP and TPP have stronger and more systemized dispersion abilities than does the B&R; the RCEP and TPP are capable of enhancing member dynamics. Although the B&R is also capable of this, members must establish bilateral relations with China. Therefore, achieving a consistent pace among all members is extremely difficult. Regarding members' attitudes toward rules, members of the RCEP believe in the rules at each level and anticipate the collective governance of the rules. When a layer expands, members are willing to respect the initial rules of said layer and expect the new rules to expand their interests. TPP members respect the rules and are willing to work to expand them; however, the priority of the rules changes concurrently with the power structure of the system. The B&R currently exhibits bilateral progression or the regional expansion of FTZ connections, and thus it constitutes an embedded multilateral system. In this context, "embedded" refers to the national interests of all cooperating parties. The advantage of embedded multilateralism is that the content of the B&R system becomes increasingly tolerant and diversified. However, if rules lack unification, problems will arise in future multilateral efforts.

There is no single model or form of global trade governance, nor is there a single structure or set of structures. It is a broad, dynamic, complex process of interactive decision- making that is constantly evolving and responding to changing circumstances. We believe the B&R is a set of trade governance theories based on Chinese philosophies and wisdom. The initiative is highly relevant in global governance. It will involve reforming and strengthening the existing global trade system and improving its means of collaboration among nations and interest groups. It will require a collaborative value and new governance goal.

References

Adlung, Rudolf and Mamdouh, Hamid. 2016. Plurilateral Trade Agreements: An Escape Route for the WTO? WTO Working Papers.

Bagwell, Kyle and Staiger, Robert. 2002. *The Economics of the World Trading System*. Cambridge, MA: MIT Press.

Bhagwati, Jagdish. 1996. *The World Trading System at Risk*. Beijing: Commercial Press.

Bhagwati, Jagdish. 2010. *Protectionism*. Beijing: China Renmin University Press Co., Ltd. First Edition.

The Commission on Global Governance. 2005. *Our Global Neighborhood*, The Report of the Commission on Global Governance. Oxford: Oxford University Press.

Fei, Xiaotong T. 2000. Economic Globalization and Cultural Survey of "Two Hops in the Three Grades." *Fei Xiaotong Compilation*, 17, pp. 190–202.

Friedman, Milton. 1987. *The Essence of Friedman*, edited by Kurt R. Leube. Stanford, CA: Hoover Institution.

Friedman, Thomas. 2005. *The World Is Flat: A Brief History of the Twenty-First Century*. New York: Farrar, Straus and Giroux.

Jiao, Pei. 2005. On the Characteristics of the International Politics under the Anti-Globalism Background. *Yinshan Academic Journal*, 10.

Keohane, Robert. 1994. Multilateralism: An Agenda for Research. *International Journal*, (4).

Stiglitz, Joseph. 2008. *Fair Trade for All: How Trade Can Promote Development*. Beijing: China Renmin University Press Co., Ltd., pp. 71–72.

Zhang, Yeshui. 2015. *Achieving Win–Win Cooperation along the One Belt One Road*. Beijing: China. Qui Shi, October.

Index

Note: Page numbers in italics indicate figures; those in bold indicate tables.

50; systems 47–49; trade governance principles 56–59
instrumental multilateralism 48
interdisciplinary research method 6
international advocacy 62–63

Jefferson, Thomas 17

Keohane, Robert 48
Kushan Empire 9
Kuznets, Simon 55–56

Lao, Tzu 40
League of Nations 1
liberalism 36

Manufacturing on the Move (Crandall) 37
Maritime Silk Road 11
McKenna Duties 17
most favored nation concept 35, 48
multilateralism 47–48; achieving, through connectivity 67–68; B&R embedded *69*; B&R relationship with 51; international mechanisms to promote 68; offering B&R services 67; RCEP embedded *69*; TPP arrangement *70*
mutual demise values 39

neoliberalism 18
new unbundling stage 8, 19
North American Free Trade Agreement (NAFTA) 19

Obama, Barack 20

Parthian Empire 9, 10
participation and expansion foreign policy 20
Pax Americana 21
Peel, Robert 16
plurilateral agreements 48
post-Westphalia system 20
processes, system rule 50
process theory 5–6

RCA value *see* revealed comparative advantage indices (RCA indices)
RCEP *see* Regional Comprehensive Economic Partnership (RCEP)
Reciprocal Trade Agreements Act 18
reciprocity principle 57

Regional Comprehensive Economic Partnership (RCEP) 4, 52
regionalism, B&R relationship with 52
regional trade agreements (RTAs) 48–49; evolution of *49*
Report of Manufactures (Hamilton) 17
revealed comparative advantage indices (RCA indices) 28–29; China 29, **30–31**
Roman Empire 9, 10
Ruggie, John 67–68
rules, global governance 46–47
Russia GVC Participation Index **27**, 28
Rust Belt manufacturing 37–38

Shanghai Cooperation Organisation 54
sharing principle 59
Silk Road 9–14; B&R and 23–24; civilian trade on 12–13; defined 9; government support for 11; in Han dynasty 9–11; Maritime 11; revelations of 13–14; tributary trade on 12
Smith, Adam 15, 17
south-south cooperation model 58–59
special and differential treatment (SDT) 58
Staiger, Robert 57
Stiglitz, Joseph 58–59
strategic multilateralism 48
systemic multilateralism 48

Tang dynasty, tributary trade and 12
thesis, antithesis, and synthesis theory 5
three communities of common destiny 3, 45
tianxia concept 40; Fei Xiaotong view of 42–43
totalitarianism 4
TPP *see* Trans-Pacific Partnership (TPP)
trade protectionism 17–18, 21
Transatlantic Trade and Investment Partnership (TTIP) 20
Trans-Pacific Partnership (TPP) 4, 20, 35, 52
tributary trade, Silk Road 12
Trump, Donald 5, 21–22, 38, 47

UN Conference on Trade and Development (UNCTAD) 53–54
unilateral free trade policy: defined 16; of early United Kingdom 15–17
unilateralism 49

Printed in the United States
by Baker & Taylor Publisher Services